Nashville to Santiago de Compostela

cars, trains, planes, and a whole lot of walking

Robert F. Labadie

Nashville to Santiago de Compostela:

cars, planes, trains, and a whole lot of walking

Copyright © 2018 Robert F. Labadie

All rights reserved. No part of this book may be copied or reproduced in any form or by any means without the written permission of the author, except for the inclusion of brief quotations in a review.

ISBN 978-1-937081-64-5

Full Color Gift Edition ISBN 978-1-937081-62-1

Published by idjc press; visit idjc.org.

Printed and distributed by Ingram Books.

Contact the author at rflabadie@gmail.com.

Dedicated to the pilgrim within each of us.

Acknowledgements

Thanks are due the many who made this journey and this book possible. First, I am indebted to Jameson who gently pushed me to do the trek with him. I am also indebted to prior pilgrims who shared their experiences especially our parish priest, Fr. Mark Beckman, who met with Jameson and me numerous times. Fr. Mark marked up our guidebook with little notes about where to stay—he was spot on with Refuge Orisson but the vegetarian albergue in Hospital de Órbigo didn't jive with our system. But, my favorite note was his understated yet prophetic "long day" scribbled on the elevation map of Stage 26, Villafranca – O'Cebreiro! (See Chapter 16.) I am thankful to the staff of our local Recreation Equipment, Inc., better known as REI, who helped us select the right equipment and, more importantly, got us in and out of the store the weekend before we departed when we naively showed up for last minute items during their very crowded annual sale!

My work colleagues covered my absence. My family either put up with or enjoyed the long absence (I still haven't quite figured out which!) of Jameson and me in northern Spain and third son, Aidan, who was in Salamanca in central Spain on an exchange trip. Oldest son, Matthew, had just graduated from college and helped Karyn taxi Zachary around to his baseball tournaments and made her feel more secure at home. Face Timing with the home crew kept our spirits up. Lots of friends followed our blog and prayed for our safety—we are very thankful for them all.

Upon our return, Karyn surprised me with a book containing our daily blog entries. This prompted me to want to expand upon and further capture the experience in this memoir. I am very thankful for all who read and edited the drafts including my mother, a former English teacher, and Fr. Steve Wolf, who also helped make its publication possible via idjc press (www.idjc.org).

Contents

Introduction 1

Wrestling with God 3

Beginnings 11

Roncesvalles: Welcome to a hostel! 15

Zubiri, Zubiri: let's call the whole thing off 23

Pamplona: a lot of bull (or soccer!) 29

Where the wind meets the stars and beyond! 37

E-STELLA! 45

Los What-cos? Los Ar-cos 51

A train to catch in Logroño 59

The easy way to León 65

A close call with vegetarians in Hospital de Órbigo 71

Astorga, my kind of town 77

Rabanal – is that all you have? 85

Cruz de Ferro – the peak, or not… 89

Do you know the way through Ponferrada?.................. 93

The long, uphill road to Ruitelán 99

O'Cebreiro, the places you'll go 103

and the people you'll meet............................. 103

Sarria: where many join the Way 109

Portomarin: a city moved to make way for the Way. 113

Palas de Rei where the blind see..................... 117

The never ending road to Ribadiso 123

Pedrouzo: The end is near…......................... 129

Santiago de Compostela 135

Exploring Santiago... 141

Next days and weeks 145

Afterword.. 148

After-afterword 151

Closure 153

About the author

Rob Labadie was born and grew up in Pittsburgh, PA never imagining that he would hike the Camino de Santiago with one of his sons! He graduated from the University of Notre Dame with a degree in mechanical engineering and then pursued his dream of becoming a doctor at the University of Pittsburgh where he met his wife, Karyn. After graduation, they moved to Chapel Hill, North Carolina for residency and then to Nashville, Tennessee to accept a faculty position at Vanderbilt University. When the author was unexpectedly offered a pair of tickets to see his beloved Pittsburgh Steelers play in the 2009 Super Bowl, a family dilemma arose over who would join him. Oldest son Matthew got the nod leading to the establishment of a father-son trip for each son with Jameson's trip documented herein. Sons #3, Aidan, and #4, Zachary, have yet to decide upon their adventures…

Introduction

It's amazing how little life we human beings actually live. The vast majority of us travel less than 500 miles from our place of birth instead living vicariously through television and the Internet. That's a real shame because the world is so big and beautiful and realizing how small we are in comparison is an enlightening experience.

I've been given a great gift. In the summer of 2017 I had the opportunity to walk 300 miles of the 500 miles of the Camino de Santiago in northern Spain. I decided to write this book to summarize my experiences. It is not meant as a travel guide because there are plenty of those already available. John Brierley's *A Pilgrim's Guide to the Camino de Santiago* (Scotland: Camino Guides, 2015) is particularly comprehensive. I traveled with my then 18-year-old son Jameson who motivated the trip as his "special trip with dad," a tradition which began when I unexpectedly got two tickets to the 2009 Super Bowl and took our oldest son, Matthew, much to the disappointment of his three younger brothers! At that point I promised each of them a special trip with Dad. Little did I know that I would have to own up to it with a 300 mile hike with son #2!

2

During our journey, I wrote an email to our parish priest who hiked the entirety of the Camino in 2014. In that email I stated that describing the Camino is like describing being married, having a kid, or being ordained a priest—the experience cannot be suitably described but only experienced. I hope this book motivates you to experience your own Camino whether in northern Spain or central Tennessee or wherever the good Lord leads you.

Chapter 1
Wrestling with God

The famous Greek writer Nikos Kazantzakis, in his memoir *Report to Greco*, relates a story of an elderly monk being questioned by a younger monk about his continuing struggles against the devil, to which the old monk replies "No, I used to, when I was younger, but now I have grown old and tired and the devil has grown old and tired with me. I leave him alone and he leaves me alone." "So your life is easy then?" replied the young monk. "Oh no," replied the monk, "it's much worse, now I wrestle with God!" This story illustrates that in early stages of spirituality we struggle with temptations which take us away from God, but once we find our way, we struggle with answering God's will. I am sure it was God's will for me to hike the Camino, but I also know that I wrestled with Him before and during the journey.

Prior to the Camino I was a very successful otolaryngologist living a perfectly happy life married to a wonderful woman with whom we had four fantastic sons. I was a tenured full professor at a top tier academic medical center, author of well over one hundred scientific papers, multiple textbook chapters, coauthor of a textbook, and recipient of multiple grants from the National Institutes of

Health (NIH). But, at the age of 50, I was yearning for something else although it took me a while to figure that out.

I was stuck in a rut in the road. I went to work and was productive and came home to a wonderful family life with a nice dinner. I swam at least three days a week for cardiovascular health and went to Catholic Mass at least two times a week. But, underneath the façade, I felt trapped. My job, while fulfilling, was sucking the life out of me. My boss, while a reasonable guy, was not so interested in helping his faculty develop into better human beings, but rather promoting his department to look better and better to outsiders. I dreaded early morning meetings which were one-way disseminations of information downward, and I despised the electronic medical record system which took me away from personal patient encounters.

Like so many physicians of my era, I wanted out but was afraid to do anything because of the economic benefits of my job to my family including a recent college graduate, an incoming college student, a rising high school junior, and the delight of our family—a 10 year old son who would be in school for another 12 years! I thought I needed the economic stability to keep the ship upright. Little did I realize I was the impaired captain headed for the iceberg. I had tried many other activities seeking something else, not even sure what that something else was. We bought a lake house as a family retreat. I took a six week sabbatical and wrote a textbook. I went back to night school and got my Masters of Management in Healthcare. I invented and tried to commercialize an anticipatory Christmas clock. I was recruited to become chair of other ENT programs. I took Google's *Search Inside Yourself* course. I took socially acceptable drugs—coffee to get me up in the morning and wine to put me down at night.

My wonderful wife Karyn put up with it all. She would listen to me complain about my situation yet celebrate my accomplishments. Having been together for over 25 years, she knows me maybe better than I know myself. Being much more spiritually gifted than myself, she encouraged me to keep looking and directed me to deeper discoveries of our faith. I think the wake-up call came when out third son, Aidan, who is perhaps more like me than any of the others, asked me why I wasn't happy. I really thought I appeared happy, but kids see the truth, and in his youthful naiveté he knew something was amiss.

I kept trying. I read spiritual books, perhaps the best of which being *Holy Longing: The Search for a Christian Spirituality* by Ronald Rolheiser. Through his book I realized that I was trying to do too much. I realized I wasn't trusting God to work in my life. I thought I could do it all—take care of the family and prepare for the inevitable—but I couldn't. About this time our then senior in high school, Jameson, asked me if I would be willing to walk the Camino with him during the summer after his graduation from high school. I was shocked and didn't know what to say. I was familiar with *The Way* from the movie of the same name but didn't find a multiple hundred mile hike staying in hostels so appealing. He continued to inquire over the ensuing months asking for this to be his "special trip with dad" (his older brother Matthew got an unexpected trip to the Super Bowl to see the Pittsburgh Steelers beat the Arizona Cardinals in the 2009 Super Bowl which lead to my promise to each son that they would get a special trip with Dad). My wife Karyn pushed me over the edge telling me that 18-year olds don't typically ask to spend so much time with their fathers and this opportunity might not come around again. Listening to her excellent advice, I reluctantly agreed.

What happened next was pretty predictable—excitement about the upcoming trip, including purchasing lots of equipment from expensive outdoor equipment companies given for birthday and Christmas presents. Perhaps the point of no return was purchasing airline tickets which happened approximately three months before the trip. At that point I knew we were committed. This was followed by attempts to train, including early morning hikes in the park near our house in Nashville, when I would put 15 pound weights in a backpack and hike for about two hours before work. True to my engineering roots, I tried to figure out precise combinations of clothing and equipment I would need. I tried various combinations of socks—I found that lightweight wool liners with thicker outer wool socks worked best for me. I tried various hydration systems—I did not like the "platypus" systems because I tended to over-drink from them bloating my belly and settled on dual 750 ml bottles stowed in side pockets of my backpack. I downloaded books to read on my iPhone. I tossed and turned on whether to take two or three pairs of clothes—I settled on two pairs of outer wear and three pairs of underwear.

Also happening at this time was an incredible amount of work to meet self-imposed deadlines, including submission of a very large NIH grant and working with colleagues to cover my nearly three week absence. I felt that if I successfully did all this work I deserved to take this trip. And, to top it all off, three weeks before the trip our oldest son, Matthew, graduated from college and two weeks before the trip Jameson, my walking partner, graduated from high school. To say that this was the perfect time to go on such an adventure would be a stretch, but I'm not sure there ever is a perfect time. Or, maybe, anytime is the perfect time.

As the scheduled departure time decreased from weeks to hours, I became more and more nervous. What was I doing? What was I getting myself into? The day before our departure was my wife's 49th birthday, and we had a lovely Sunday afternoon cookout following which we watched a 2017 movie, *The Shack*, about a grieving father who lost his daughter to a horrible death and meets with the tripartite God (Father, Son, and Holy Spirit) during his healing. I made an error and did not eat dinner that night after the midday cookout. This error led to restless sleep and more wrestling with God. I felt sick physically and emotionally. I begged God to stop me from going if something bad was going to happen, e.g., a heart attack. I awoke early and sat outside wallowing in my self-pity. When Karyn awoke I hugged her and cried like a schoolboy afraid to go to school on the first day. She gave me a pep talk. I called my elderly parents who also gave me a pep talk. I revisited what would happen if my parents would pass away while we were hiking. My father, who introduced me to backpacking as a child, told me he felt that he was joining us on this grand adventure and wanted us to finish the hike no matter what. I tearfully said goodbye to everyone at home and we drove to the airport.

On the way to the airport – Jameson, left, Zachary, middle, and the author on the right.

For those pilgrims starting their pilgrimage in Europe, getting to Saint Jean Pied-de-Port is relatively easy. For those outside Europe, it's a journey before the journey. We flew from Nashville to Detroit; during the flight I lost the chest strap for my backpack which I took as an ominous sign. Next, we flew to Paris. Following this, we caught a commuter flight to Biarritz, France. On that flight we met a couple from Seattle who were also traveling to hike the Camino—they commented on how small our packs were, and we commented on how large theirs were! The train service was on strike the day we arrived so we split a taxi with a pilgrim from Australia for the 50 km drive to Saint Jean. We checked into our hotel and were buzzing with anticipation. We went to the Pilgrim headquarters to receive our credentials—a passport of sorts that gets stamped on the way to document that you are completing the pilgrimage—and made some last-minute purchases, including trekking poles which we would find to be essential.

Perhaps the only thing I forgot that I wish I would've taken was a small travel cribbage board. Cribbage is a very old card game with scoring similar to poker but with interesting twists. First, the deal alternates between players on successive hands with the dealer being given a second hand comprised of cards discarded from both the dealer's and non-dealer's hands. An additional card is turned over from the deck which is in everybody's hand including the third hand, the crib (the **dealer's** bonus hand from the discards). Following the deal, cards are played and points are awarded. After play, the hands are counted with the dealer getting to count both his hand and "the crib." Scores are kept on a peg board of 4 rows of 30 holes with the first one to reach 121 (twice up and back) the winner. We have been playing cribbage in my family for years, and I wanted to teach Jameson on this trip but forgot my travel board. Instead, he learned from an iPhone app on the plane ride over, and we bought a deck of cards in Saint Jean for one Euro and kept score with pencil and paper. We played our first game the night before we embarked on the Camino—I won but he put in a good showing.

10

Before retiring for the night, both Jameson and I found letters tucked away in our backpacks from Karyn. In her letter to me, Karyn let me know that—short of marrying me and raising a family—she was never more certain of anything other than Jameson and I doing the Camino. She referenced *The Shack's* central theme, God's incredible love for each of us no matter what. It was reassuring. We stayed awake long enough to overcome the time change and slept well adjusting to local time and overcoming "jet lag."

Chapter 2
Beginnings

Life is made up of meetings and partings.
- Kermit the Frog playing Bob Cratchit in *The Muppet Christmas Carol* as quoted from Barb Higgins' funeral

The next morning we arose bright-eyed and bushy-tailed. We had breakfast and were out the door by 8:30 am stopping to take pictures in front of the gate marking the official starting point. It was a beautiful morning. The setting was similar to *The Sound of Music* with rolling French hills in the background. When I couldn't remember the lyrics to *The Sound of Music* Jameson sang the *Fun Song* from *SpongeBob Square Pants*:

We begin!

F is for friends who do stuff together
U is for you and me
N is for anywhere and anytime at all;
Down here in the deep blue sea!

We laughed. I hadn't laughed like that in months. It felt great! (Jameson would comment days later that he hadn't heard me laugh like that in years—I think he was right.)

We passed a young woman walking barefoot with a toddler. I thought she was a local but would come to find out that she was a fellow pilgrim. In my journal that night I wrote about the ruts in the road that I encountered on this first day. I reflected on how easy it is to get into a routine and how difficult it is to get oneself out of that routine. Some of my routines in my pre-Camino life were good and some were bad, yet it would be important to get out of the ruts.

Hiking through the Pyrenees on Day 1 – Jameson on the left and the author on the right.

We arrived at our first day destination, Orisson, just before 12:30 pm and only about 4 hours into our hike. It reminded me of a ski chalet with people sitting out on the patio drinking beer and eating snacks. We ordered lunch and a Basque cake, a crumb cake with almond tart in the middle. It was our favorite dessert of the entire trip! At about 2 pm the proprietor took us to our rooms—dormitory style with four sets of bunk beds and shared bathrooms without seats on the commodes. We were given a token for five minutes of water in the shower which worked as long as you soaped beforehand. Without Wi-Fi they had a great sign which read "We don't have Wi-Fi, talk to each other." We visited with fellow pilgrims from all around the world including Australia and Brazil. We played cribbage. I journaled. About 4-5 pm in the afternoon the barefoot woman with the toddler checked in and got a standing ovation.

Dinner was served promptly at 7 pm and included water, wine, bread, French onion soup, chicken, and a vegetable stew. It was delicious. We ate community style. After dinner, we stood up and introduced ourselves. Many countries and continents were represented including Australia, Europe, Japan, North America, and South American. After dinner, a fellow American pilgrim and bunkmate, Eric, came up to talk to us and explained he was a surgeon from Colorado traveling with his wife. They were walking in sports sandals at the recommendation of a good friend who had completed the Camino. They were shipping, or portaging, their packs ahead each day to make the hike more pleasant and recommended we do the same—we passed. We also ran into a group of three Americans, two of whom were hiking a stage of the Camino in support of their friend who planned to hike the entire Camino. He worked for the Pittsburgh Penguins organization. This grabbed our attention because at the time our home team, the Nashville Predators, were playing the Pittsburgh Penguins in the Stanley Cup finals! We spoke briefly and then headed off to bed by 10 pm—just about sunset, but it didn't get really dark until about midnight.

The first night of sleeping was difficult. I forgot to use my earplugs, and our bunkmates were snoring (I'm sure I was as well!). I had to get up to use the restroom multiple times throughout the evening. We forgot to open the window and it got rather warm. But, we made it through the first night with everybody getting up about 6:30 am. We had a very simple breakfast of toast and jam and purchased bag lunches to carry with us. We were "off" or, more correctly, "up" because the peak laid quite a ways up the road!

Sunrise in the Pyrenees.

Chapter 3

Roncesvalles: Welcome to a hostel!

Many pilgrims decide not to stop at Orisson, instead preferring to hike the first day in a single 25 km stretch over the Pyrenees into the Spanish town of Roncesvalles. At the recommendation of our parish priest, we stopped at Orisson and it was the right thing for us. The morning climb from Orisson to Roncesvalles consisted of a climb of another 1500 m in elevation (in addition to the 700 m of elevation we

A monument to Mary in the Pyrenees.

climbed on day one). The scenery was very similar to that in the Smokey Mountains in Tennessee. We saw monuments to the Blessed Virgin Mary. One German couple had brought a candle in a jar and left it lit at the most famous shrine near the top. We stopped and had snacks at a trailer manned by a local and got a "Thibault stamp"—the name of the son of a friend of ours from Nashville. We met Norman from Nottingham and his traveling companion, Gary from Birmingham, who was on his third Camino. When asked why he had chosen to do so many Caminos, his only response was "sheer stupidity." We had conversations about English and American politics, immigration, the Brexit, and the upcoming American Presidential election.

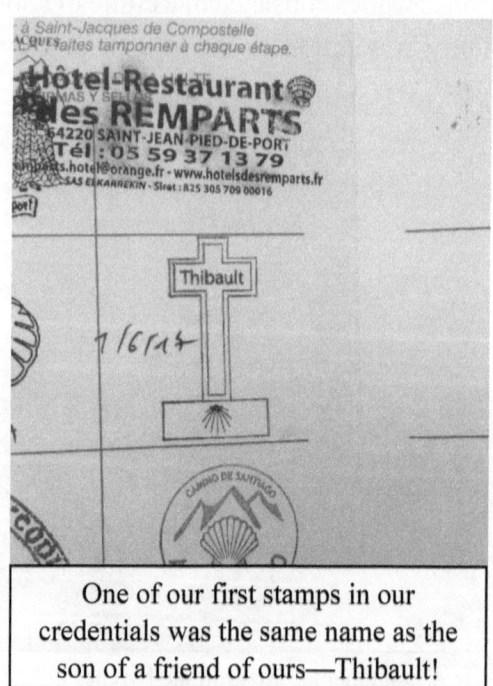

One of our first stamps in our credentials was the same name as the son of a friend of ours—Thibault!

Jameson had so much energy he wanted to explore a rock outcrop about 200 yards off the road and had to tiptoe around extensive sheep dung to reach it. I wisely sat down and ate my sandwich. We left the narrow winding road to ascend on an earthen tract which went through a narrow pass—the highest point we would reach—and passed by an old stone shelter which our guidebook indicated could be used for emergency shelter. We then started walking on a leaf covered track which had on its left side a steep earthen embankment and on the right a steep drop off lined with beautiful trees. We met Kate, a twenty-something from Texas, who was in between her job as a paralegal and law school. Kate had done lots of adventure trips like this in the past. She was through hiking from Saint Jean directly to Roncesvalles and had an accelerated plan to complete the Camino in 28 days instead of the typical 33. As a parent, I asked how her parents handled this—she said not so great but she checked in with them every couple days. She told me how great it was that I was doing this with my son. (Actually, I think she said it was "cool"—more to come on that later.) We crossed over the France-Spain border (one country down, one to go!) and continued hiking with Kate and were passed by dirt bike riders at one point. We came to a high point with emergency Wi-Fi if needed (thank God we did not!), and were faced with a choice of a longer gradual descent or a shorter steep descent. Norman from Nottingham was going steep—he wanted today's hike to be done. We wisely chose the gradual descent, which was steep enough. At about this point we could see the monastery of Roncesvalles, our destination for the day, in the valley. It looked so inviting, and I recall being very excited. The descent continued for a couple more hours. We finally entered an enchanting forest with a stream running along one side and could see the gates of the monastery!

Roncesvalles in the distance.

Immediately upon arrival to Roncesvalles, we were met by a man with a video camera. He told us he was a Spanish teacher from a small American college and was doing a documentary on the Camino but was working backwards from Santiago. He asked if he could interview us. Six hours into our second day and euphoric about the adventure, we agreed. He asked mostly standard questions, including "Why are you doing this?" Jameson told him about his exposure to the Camino in Spanish class through the movie *The Way* and his desire to deepen his spirituality. I told him about how Jameson had asked me repeatedly to do this as his "special dad trip" and how my wife encouraged me. His question continued to haunt me for days if not weeks to come. (A similar question is posed in Brierley's guide book for pre-trip reflection, pp. 36-38.)

We checked in about 2 pm for 20 Euros each including dinner and were told to come back at 4 pm. We went to get lunch at one of the cafes in town and ended up sitting with the Spanish school teacher and another pilgrim who was a former professional tennis player and on the board of trust of a Southern university. We discussed healthcare and education. Exhausted, we excused ourselves to check in and perhaps get some rest. One of the attendants at the hostel, who we later found out was from the Danish order of Saint James, took us to our beds. Sleeping accommodations, which were bunkbeds, were arranged in groups of four with about 100 in any given open area. We quickly realized that one showered and then worried about getting laundry done and then rested for the next day.

A quick aside here re accommodations. There are many ways to do the Camino, including camping, albergues (hostels), pensions (rural hotels), and traditional hotels. Camping sites are available but often without facilities. Camping necessitates that one carry additional weight (e.g. tent, backpack). Albergues are either run by the town (municipal) or are private and consist of shared living accommodations with as few as four but often dozens if not hundreds of beds in common spaces with shared bathrooms. Pensions are rooms to rent, often from private homes, and typically have shared bathrooms. Hotels provide simple lodging in private rooms with private or shared bathrooms. Costs increase with each option but are typically inexpensive—an albergue may be free or suggested donation of up to 20 Euros, a pension typically runs 20-30 Euros, and a hotel 30-40 Euros for a single and 40-60 Euros for a double. Many pilgrims feel that albergues are the purist way to experience the Camino because the experience is shared with others, and many young pilgrims camp or stay at hostels/albergues to minimize costs. As I realized a bit later on, Kate thought I was "cool" because I was doing the albergue experience with my 18 year-old son!

Back to the Roncesvalles albergue. I did okay with the shower but then freaked out when I realized that this was going to become the norm for the next three weeks. Jameson tried to calm me down by playing cribbage, but it didn't work. I wanted to be in control. I went online to book a hotel in Pamplona, only a couple days hike away. I emailed about availability for the next day in Zubiri. I could figure this out.

I could find us a better place to stay. But, God had other plans. First off, I booked the wrong date for Pamplona. Little did I know that Real Madrid and Jeventus were playing for the European League Championship the night I was trying to book, and there were no rooms available. I called in panic to cancel only to realize that the cancellation penalty was equal to the cost of the room (79 Euros—thanks for nothing booking.com and Hotel Castillo de Javier!). The person in the next town, Zubiri, responded via email in Spanish that they didn't have any more private rooms but had some bunkbeds left. I imposed on one of our "bunkmates," Christian from Barcelona, to respond to the email, which he did reserving for us a bunkbed in Zubiri.

I settled down a little bit for dinner which was a very efficient affair with two sittings in three different restaurants, all of the same pilgrim menu with two choices for starters, two choices for main dish, as well as water and wine. We were seated with an elderly French couple who didn't speak a lick of English. Through various modes of communication we learned they were finishing their Camino which they had started years ago. I think they were in their late 60's/early 70's and were staying in the same accommodations as we were. I looked around and noticed a lot of other older adults doing the same thing. I felt embarrassed about complaining.

On the way back to the dormitory I saw a docent from the Danish Saint James Society. He had done two Caminos and now volunteered for two weeks every summer at this albergue. I asked him questions about accommodations along the way. He told me that the Camino provides but not always in the ways that one wants. I told him my son and I had reversed roles with my son being more a parent than I was at the moment. He said that was not an uncommon experience. We went to Mass, all in Spanish except for a blessing afterwards in many languages. Preparing for bed I noticed that that the "faith" charm one of my kids had made in vacation bible school and that I had attached to my backpack had fallen off—I had literally lost my faith!—how prophetic of what I was experiencing. We settled in for sleep, but this time I used earplugs! The next morning I realized one of the unwritten advantages of hostels—no one wants to stay another night and everyone gets moving early. We were out of there by 7 am sharp!

Chapter 4

Zubiri, Zubiri: let's call the whole thing off

We left Roncesvalles and took pictures by the famous sign (Santiago de Compostela 790 km). I recall an excited pilgrim—a middle-aged or older Asian woman—screaming "I love the Camino!" and then stating loudly that this was her 3rd Camino and the people kept her coming

Only 790 kilometers to go!

back. We stopped about 1-2 miles outside town at a café and had breakfast. I quickly learned that *bocadillos* (sandwiches) can be eaten any time of day! I also realized that there were many more options for sleeping than I had imagined. We did not have to stay in the large albergues, there were plenty of pensions and even hotels!

We passed public toilets, crossed a small stream, and headed into the countryside. It was a beautiful day. Jameson and I passed time saying a Rosary and then talking with each other and fellow pilgrims. Jameson ended up walking with a twenty-something from Italy discussing current events and spirituality. Conversations on the Camino quickly get "deep." I think this happens because the entry cost for being there is so high both financially and emotionally leading many to share things they might refrain from sharing in pre-Camino normal life. This happened repeatedly to both Jameson and me.

At Alto de Erro we crossed a highway (the N-135), where taxis lurch, preying on weak souls who want a ride to Zubiri. Also, there is a trailer café that was substantial enough to warrant mention in our guidebook. We had something to eat, got a stamp for our credentials, and admired

Looking for a spouse?

the interesting box of undergarments and the sign stating "Looking for husband or wife? Leave here you underwear, magic works!" Interestingly enough, the box was filled mostly with bras.

We then embarked on a steep decline—300 m over 3 km. Descents are often more dangerous than ascents because descents are when blisters form. We carefully retied our boots the way the associate from the outdoor equipment store suggested and pressed on. Finally, Zubiri came into view. Many pilgrims press on another 5 km to Larrasoaña on this day's hike so they can have more time in Pamplona (the next day's stop), but we were ready for a break and hoped we had better accommodations waiting. We crossed the beautiful medieval bridge over the river (rio) Agua and,

The view from the deck of the albergue in Zubiri.

seemingly amazingly, the albergue we had called was the first building on our left! And, it looked nice! I rang the buzzer and the young gentleman answered the door and showed us the bunk room—5 sets of bunks and 2 bathrooms—and only two other pilgrims had checked in, cousins from South Korea who were being educated in the United States. We picked some prime bunks, took amazing showers (no 5 minute limit here!) and went to find food.

After a very nice meal, we took a siesta—what a civilized idea!—and started playing cards (cribbage) on the lovely deck looking out over the río Agua. And then it happened. Three pilgrims barged onto the deck and quickly pulled out their cell phones and cigarettes—or perhaps it was first cigarettes and then cell phones. Our tranquil scene had been violated. Our first unspoken impression was that our idyllic albergue had just been desecrated. We tried to continue playing cards but our moods were clearly altered. We decided to get ready to try to find dinner so we went downstairs to the bunkroom (in the back of my mind I also wanted to make sure that these intruders were not messing with our stuff!). We went in the bunk room and found the trio working on a backpack repair. They spoke with German accents. I said "hi" and they introduced themselves as Jordi, 19, Robin, 20, and Frank, age unspecified but late 30's/early 40's. Jordi was a rehabilitation nurse from Belgium. He graduated from high school being the equivalent of a licensed practical nurse (LPN) and worked taking care of patients in rehabilitation hospitals. His waist belt on his back pack had broken the day before, and he had hiked the entire day with only shoulder straps. (For those of you who backpack regularly, you know how devastating this is because the weight of a backpack should be held on one's hips with the shoulder straps only preventing forward lurch of the pack.) His shoulders were red and sore. He had bought a replacement belt in Zubiri, which had a surprisingly complete outdoors store and was trying to fix it. I leaned over to help. Robin then introduced himself and the trio asked us if we wanted to join them for dinner. WHAT?!? Join them?!? While I immediately thought that the evening would quickly degenerate with us doing late night shots of tequila or something else, we didn't have any other offers and—not wanting to offend our bunkmates—we skeptically agreed.

The trio had met another pilgrim, Pablo, an early-retired investment banker from Mexico, whose personal life had taken a toll from his career. He was on a 6 month round-the-world trip to try to find himself. Being from Mexico, he spoke fluent Spanish and found a restaurant and ordered for us. Most meals on the Camino are simple and cheap. A starter, main course, bread, wine, water, and dessert all for 10 Euros or less. We had such a meal—can't remember exactly what we ate—but vividly recall the conversation when we all got to know each other. Robin was a 20 year old former perfume sales agent who was directly out of casting from *Sound of Music* complete with Tyrolean hat. He had hiked the entire Camino three years before, almost being robbed in the Meseta (the high desert plateau, 800 m above sea level, where distances can be very deceiving); he had to outrun some youths with knives who wanted his expensive backpack and fancy hiking boots. Jordi, the LPN, had a very short haircut, sideburns and goatee making him look like a stereotypical "skinhead." Frank was an alternate lifestyle Pilates and yoga instructor who was from Germany but now resided abroad with his boyfriend who was still married with children (his boyfriend's wife was slowly coming to terms with the situation). His boyfriend was joining him in León. They learned about Jameson and me. We talked American politics (Frank was shocked to hear that I, a doctor living in the southern United States, was a moderate). The vibe at the table was incredible.

The evening ended with us getting some Belgium beer (Robin and Jordi were very proud of their country's best export!) and reconvening on the deck at the albergue to try to fix Jordi's backpack. I offered the folded up duct tape I had, and we were able to accomplish a pretty effective field repair. We retired to bed relatively early. I slept well but awoke a couple times to use the bathroom. Jameson and I wanted to leave early to beat the heat, and we left Robin, Jordi, and Frank behind, promising that we would meet again in the next town but pretty sure that we wouldn't. I had very mixed feelings about them. Their appearance, a bit scary, belied their actions, helpful and sincere. In my pre-Camino life, I wouldn't have spent much time with "them" but here they were pilgrims just like us. Jameson liked them but agreed they were a bit "off."

Chapter 5

Pamplona: a lot of bull (or soccer!)

After a decent night of sleep—I remembered to use the earplugs but the bathroom emanated a weird odor—we got up early and left by 6:30 am leaving Robin, Jordi, and Frank behind. The day was somewhat overcast but without serious rain and had only drizzle. The next couple of miles were through a rural industrial park including what appeared to be several stone quarries. We passed through Larrasoaña where a large cohort of pilgrims had stayed the night before, and the trail got a bit busier. Familiar faces appeared including some older pilgrims who, quite frankly, I was amazed were still walking. We hiked through beautiful fields next to río Arga. Jameson found a lovely spot to get closer to the river. We stopped and had brunch at Café la Parade in Zuriain expecting Frank, Jordi, and Robin to catch us, but they didn't.

Jameson was having some problems with his bowels, and about an hour after brunch he needed to use the bathroom urgently. We were in the middle of nowhere. I saw a couple home businesses where we tried to stop, but everything was closed due to the early Saturday hour. We were hitting panic mode when we turned a corner and saw

Unexpected bathroom building (and a happy Jameson!).

some fishermen on the river and I asked them if there was a *baño* close by and they pointed us to a park bathroom 100 yards away that served its purpose quite well! My mind raced back to the Dutch volunteer in Roncesvalles: the Camino provides, maybe not the way you expect, but it always provides!

Hiking along, we came upon Donna and Dell, the pilgrims from Seattle who we met on the flight from Paris to Biarritz who had the monstrous backpacks. Donna looked miserable; she clearly had an upper respiratory infection or sinus infection and was struggling to carry on. They had hiked to Roncesvalles in a single day and were one day ahead of us but then stopped in Zubiri for two nights to try and recover from her cold. They were planning to go to a physician in Pamplona. I told her that they had just found a physician and pulled antibiotics out of my pack. They were very grateful, and Donna started the medicine right away promising to spend an extra day in Pamplona to recover. The Camino provides!

As we got closer to Pamplona, we walked by a very busy highway, and there was a vista of the city ahead of us. It looked so close, but I was learning that looks were deceiving! We walked through one of Pamplona's suburbs and thought we were there. We weren't. We struggled to stay on the Way with sparse Camino signs competing with billboards and other city markers. We passed by a festival. We found a banking machine and withdrew some Euros.

Pamplona in the distance. (Caution: objects appear closer than they really are on the Camino!)

(Whew!—This was the first use of my bank card in Europe and we didn't have a backup plan if it didn't work!) We pushed on thinking the city center of Pamplona was around the next corner and then the next and then the next.

Finally, we crossed an ancient bridge into Pamplona but then got even more lost! We took a left where we should've taken a right and saw the German albergue that Robin had told us about where he stayed on his last Camino and highly recommended. My gut told me to go in and ask for a room, but I didn't after a pilgrim who was staying there came out and looked a little rough. We saw a very large wall and next to it what appeared to be an elevator. People were taking the elevator up to the old city center. Being pigheaded we walked up the hill instead and got even more lost! The sky was now beginning to darken, we didn't know where we were, and we didn't have accommodations for the night. And, this was the night of the European football championship between Real Madrid and Juventus so we were uncertain if we were going to find a place to sleep.

We wandered around the city looking for markers and asking people if they knew where the Camino was. Amazingly few knew. We found this very common in major metropolitan areas—familiarity with the Way is much less common than in rural areas. We finally made it to the center of the city and the Cathedral and saw a man drinking a glass of wine outside a hotel. I asked him if he was a pilgrim. He said he was and was staying at this hotel. I asked if they had availability and the proprietor said defiantly "no" and to try the municipal albergue. This was not what I wanted to hear.

But, given that we had no other options, we found the municipal albergue, Jesús y María, and checked in. It was very similar to the albergue in Roncesvalles being a converted church with hundreds of beds dormitory style. The first beds we were assigned to were so close to their neighbors that if one rolled over he would be in his neighbor's bed. I freaked out. I found a little nook where there were four bunkbeds and asked the attendant to change our beds to these which he graciously did. No sooner had we gotten done with our showers than Robin, Jordan, and Frank rolled in, wearing their ponchos, and relating a similar story of getting lost going through the city!

Our accommodations in the municipal albergue in Pamplona. On the left the open nave of the church with rows of bunkbeds, and on the right the little alcove we shared with two other pilgrims.

We agreed to go out for dinner and started wandering the ancient streets of Pamplona through which the bulls would be running the following month and bought slices of pizza from a street stand. We walked to a city square where they were setting up a viewing party for the European football championship. SWAT teams and paddy wagons were there as well, preparing for the expected rowdy celebrations. We grabbed a beer and Jameson had one of the thickest hot chocolates any of us had ever seen! (We postulated it was pudding!) I got online and looked up the lyrics to Bruce Springsteen's *Thunder Road* which had been running in my head throughout the day's hike. The group

Jameson and Frank enjoying pizza in Pamplona.

wanted to get tapas, and Pablo found an upscale restaurant where we ate. We ordered what we thought was the right amount of food, but the waiter brought us three times the amount! Amazingly, or maybe not amazingly given the calories we were burning every day, we finished all of it. Jameson and I went to the 8 pm pilgrim's Mass at the beautiful Cathedral and then settled in for a relatively early night wanting to shake the dust of Pamplona from our feet early the next morning.

We met our alcove mates including a German woman who was doing a pilgrimage from her hometown in Germany to Santiago in two weeks blocks over the past five years. She told us she had walked about 700 km to date and showed us her credentials with pages and pages of stamps. She was not sure how far she would get this two-week block but thought she would make it somewhere close to León. While Jameson appeared to sleep well, I was awakened at 3 am by celebrating soccer fans who decided that the alley just outside our alcove was the perfect place to relive the events of last night. I think they went to bed at 5 am and I finally fell asleep only to be awakened by the lights being turned on at 6 am pushing pilgrims out the door. If I could've quit at this point, I would have. I was physically and emotionally exhausted. I did not like staying in albergues. I wasn't experiencing the spiritual transformation that I was expecting. It's a good thing there weren't a lot of good options to get home, or I think I would've bailed.

Jameson in front of the Cathedral in Pamplona.

Chapter 6

Where the wind meets the stars and beyond!

We grabbed a quick breakfast and headed out of town as a cohesive group with Robin, Frank, and Jordi. We weaved through downtown Pamplona and into the outskirts, walking around a beautiful college campus and then began our assent to Alto del Perdon, which Robin warned us was going to be difficult. We had brunch about 3 to 5 miles outside of Pamplona where Frank used his "big" knife to cut our *bocadillos*. The trail got more rural and started to trend significantly uphill. The walk was beautiful but physically demanding. We met a schoolteacher from Los Angeles who was doing the Camino with his wife. He was an African-American man built like a linebacker and he was making quicker progress than his wife. Every few minutes they

Frank's small knife is no match for this *bocadillo*!

would volley to each other with the man shouting "can't stop" and the wife responding "won't stop." They were so impressed with Pamplona that they had booked a train ticket from Santiago back to the city to see the running of the bulls. (More on them later.)

The weather was now beginning to become overcast, and as we hiked up to the peak of the mountain we came closer and closer to large wind turbines. The sound emanating from them was hauntingly beautiful. We passed an Italian priest who had concelebrated Mass in Roncesvalles and Pamplona. We tried to engage him in conversation, but he was seeking solitude. We finally reached the top where there are relatively famous figurines cut in steel representing pilgrims from various ages. There is a plaque to the chapel that once stood on the spot, and legend

Where the wind meets the stars.

has it that pilgrims who reach this peak will have their sins forgiven and be admitted to heaven if they die on the way to Santiago which apparently was not an unusual occurrence in the Middle Ages and before. We admired the view and snapped a couple pictures.

Just upon descent, the rain started. Fortunately, we were prepared and pulled out our rain gear. The descent was difficult, rocky, and now slick. The rain intensified. We passed a woman who had no raincoat and poor footwear. Jameson offered her his raincoat. She refused. We carried on. We discovered that Jameson's raincoat wasn't actually waterproof even though the label indicated it was. We came upon a café where seemingly every pilgrim was stopping to get out of the rain. Robin, Jordi, and Frank were there and had a table where they had saved us seats. We ordered

Looking back at the summit where the wind meets the stars.

sandwiches, coffee, and hot chocolate and warmed up. Christian, who had shared the quad of bunks in the albergue in Roncesvalles, was there. After a much needed 45 minute to one hour break we set off again in the pouring rain which was literally coming down at a 45° angle. We passed a hedgerow that provided wonderful shelter from the rain and wind. Shortly afterwards, the rain stopped.

Jameson passing through the eye of the needle.

We still had a way to go to make the next town. We hiked on, meeting two men from Croatia who were doing the Camino in stages. They told me they were staying exclusively in private double rooms. I was jealous. We went through Obanos, which had an eye of the needle monument, and from the hill in town we looked back at the place where the wind meets the stars engulfed in clouds. We pressed on. The Croatian pilgrims were having an impromptu picnic lunch and offered food to us as we passed. The generosity of pilgrims was ever present. In short order, we arrived at Puente La Reina. I wanted to stop at the first reasonable hotel, but Robin said the last hostel was the best even though it was up a hill. Trusting him, we walked through town. I stopped at a market and bought a couple bottles of wine, cold cuts, cheese, and bread for a snack for the five of us for a total cost of about 8 Euros. We poked our head into what appeared to be a dilapidated old church, Iglesia de Santiago, but was one of the most gorgeous Spanish churches we had

Iglesia de Santiago.

yet seen. As with most of the other churches, the altarpiece was extensive and gilded. Even Frank, who said he hadn't been to church in years but was perhaps motivated by us to enter, was impressed.

We pressed on through the edge of town and crossed the oldest bridge in Spain built by the Romans before Christ. Robin kept insisting that the hostel was just ahead. After we crossed the bridge, we started up a hill of at least one kilometer on a lane that never seemed to end. We were motivated by promises of a swimming pool and a country setting. But, when we arrived, we found the pool was not yet open (summer did not officially begin until June 21) and was filled with murky, muddy water. We were told that we could have one of the rooms with five bunkbeds in it to ourselves for 10 Euros apiece. This seemed like a good deal and we took it. It still had shared bathrooms, but they were sizeable. We washed and dried clothes. Jordi told us to put newspaper in our hiking boots to wick away moisture; we did, and it worked well. We all caught up on journaling and, with good Wi-Fi, called loved ones. That night Frank worked some of his massage magic on our sore feet, applying compressive wraps and teaching us stretches using a small exercise ball. I think it helped, and it was something that we did for the rest of the trip. Robin had a friend who was driving to a national park close to where we were and was planning to meet us for dinner but had travel delays, so we ate at the hostel which was very reasonable. We slept well that night. Jameson said it reminded him of summer camp, and I agreed.

The oldest bridge in Spain predating Christ crossing río Arga.

Beautiful flowers abound on the Camino.

Chapter 7
E-STELLA!

After a good night's sleep we arose to find that some of our clothes were still damp from the rain the day before. I cleaned out the lint trap in the dryer and put our socks in—nothing like dry socks to boost one's spirits! Our "Godspell" group pushed off in the midst of a very delicate mist. We admired the ancient Spanish bridge one more time and pressed on. Jameson and I were walking with Frank whose pace better matched ours than the aggressive pace of Robin and Jordi which was often fueled by heavy metal music from their phones.

Frank talked to us about how he learned of the Camino through a famous German comedian's memoir entitled *I'm Off Then: Losing and Finding Myself on the Camino de Santiago*, by Hape (short for Hans Peter) Kerkeling. He regaled us with stories from the book but also imparted some serious concepts which we were not aware of like the concept of picking up a rock and carrying it for a while and then placing the rock on a Camino sign post or other rock pile signifying a letting go of something. I took Frank's advice and picked up a stone and, placing it on a rock pile, left behind my inferiority complex and then my anger. It was very therapeutic—lots to let go of. A short while later we came across a larger stone pile with one stone having "Buen Camino, con carino, Vanderbilt" which hit home given that I had worked at Vanderbilt since 2001.

There was a very gentle misty rain coming down despite the sun shining. Frank shared that his grandmother used to say that this meant the devil was having a party, but he now preferred to think that his grandmother—in heaven and not in hell!—was having a party. That made me think about my grandmothers, especially my Grandmother Meyer at whose house I would have lunch when walking home from grade school and my mother was out. She would always treat us to Fresca, Cheetos, and Archway cookies—such good memories! My mind raced with so many good remembrances of her.

The far reach of Vanderbilt.

We took a break for lunch in Cirauqui at a lovely little supermarket where we bought supplies including bread, cheese, and lunchmeat. As we ate, Robin, Jordi, Juan, and a new pilgrim, Juan Manuel, appeared. We danced in front of the Café El Portal, the entry to the city, and did a Rockette kick line! Jameson posted this on our blog and my mother commented via email how happy and relaxed I looked. I was surprised because I was physically exhausted and thought I looked terrible, but perhaps the trip was impacting me emotionally more than I thought.

We hiked through this lovely town and were greeted by an elderly woman wishing us "Buen Camino" as we left town. She looked to be at least 80 and I wondered how many times she had wished "Good Way" to pilgrims—probably thousands of times. We crossed an ancient Roman bridge where a pilgrim traveling with his girlfriend was hanging off, scaring his girlfriend with the nearly 50 foot drop. We crossed the highway and continued for quite some time. Robin and Jordi had hiked on ahead of us, and we met up with them at a very small roadside café that had a cave-like basement serving drinks, limited food, but no stamp for our credentials! **Robin's friend** who was supposed to meet us the night before was there with his Jack Russell Terrier. Robin and Jordi took him up on his offer to drive them to the next town, Estella, as their blisters were causing much pain. Frank, Jameson and I carried on.

The rest of the day was hot but enjoyable. We prayed, laughed, and sang. There were a couple twenty-something French girls beautifully singing French songs. I had Bruce **Springsteen's** *Thunder Road* playing in my head and, with the lyrics saved on my iPhone, turned it into a prayer with the main character being God wanting Mary (me) to join him. As I did not think the French girls would know

Impromptu Rockette kick line at city gate in Cirauqui. From left to right: author, Juan Manuel, Jameson, Frank, Pablo.

Thunder Road, I offered up *The Sound of Music's Do-Re-Me* (Doe, a deer, a female deer; Re, a drop of golden sun; Me, a name I call myself; Fa, a long, long way to run; Sew, a needle pulling thread; La, a note to follow Sew; Tea, a drink with jam and bread; which brings us back to Doe). They seemed to like it.

We rounded the corner, and the bridge crossing to Estella was on our right. We followed the old, narrow, cobblestoned streets to the city square and ran into Robin and Jordi having a beer and raving about the food at the Florida Café. I wanted to take care of accommodations and searched for the San Andreas which our parish priest had suggested. It was a non-descript small family run hotel and we found a double room for 30 or 40 Euros with a private bathroom. Right across the hall was a triple where Robin, Jordi, and Frank could stay for about the same price. They were pretty excited and we celebrated by getting lunch and then taking a siesta.

Estella's cathedral reflected in Frank's water glass.

We reconvened in the square for dinner, admired the beautiful cathedral, and topped off the meal with ice cream from a sweets shop. After dinner, Frank suggested we go into the río Ega to ease our sore muscles with the cold water. We crossed the river holding our passports and cell phone—not a great idea (thank goodness none of us fell in). We then marched in place following Frank's instructions. Jameson and I had to make a decision that night to either continue with the crew or stick with our original plan to take a train from Logroño to León. While a difficult decision, we decided to stick with our original plan so that we could summit at Cruz de Ferro. We booked our train tickets just before retiring for the day

Water therapy in río Ega in Estella (front—Jordi, back left to right – Jameson, author, Frank).

Chapter 8
Los What-cos? Los Ar-cos

The next day we left early knowing we had a LONG hike to reach Los Arcos. We crossed the bridge out of the old city and entered the bustling metropolitan area where we passed children going to school and businesses opening up. (I even think we passed the waiter from the Florida café!) Heading out of town we started an ascent and upon leaving the city limits (after being directed as to the correct way by a mom driving her child to school), we quickly came upon the Fuente del Vino, a winery with a famous free tap where pilgrims can "fortify" themselves drinking from their shells. This was Jameson's first wine outside of Mass and we all made a big deal out of it. Unfortunately, it was Monday and the monastery turned museum (the monastery closed in 1985 because of lack of vocations) was closed. We came to a fork in the road and, unlike Yogi Berra, we did not "pick it up" but rather flipped Frank's lucky coin from the Canary Islands which directed us to the right. Thankfully, the coin chose the less arduous path!

We passed a summer camp which was not yet open for the season. We stopped for brunch in Azqueta where we combined resources with Frank offering a sausage he had bought the day before, an orange Jameson and I had from the morning, and some bread and hard boiled eggs we bought in the café. The sense of community and togetherness was palpable. Hiking farther we went through Villamayor de Monjardín where we stopped at the 13th century Fountain of the Moors which was a deeply reflective spot for Jameson and Frank who meditated.

Free wine to fortify the pilgrim's journey.

13th Century Fountain of the Moors.

    Jameson and I had heard unfortunate news from Nashville that our Bishop, David Choby, had passed away. His health had been declining but he was improving. He had undergone an elective surgical procedure which he did not survive. The message from Nashville had been delayed, perhaps divinely inspired. No sooner had we gotten the news then we entered the 12th century San Andres Church with its altar adorned with lilies. It was the only church we came upon adorned by lilies, a symbol of the resurrection. I was teary eyed as I entered and contributed 1 Euro to light a candle which I placed in the middle of the candle rack attended by an elderly man. As I went to a pew to pray for

Bishop Choby's soul, I noticed the attendant moving my candle from the middle to the next spot in line. I quickly realized that while a bishop is special on earth, God treats all his children equally. My tears intensified not from grief but from joy.

We continued on through seemingly endless fields stopping at a roadside stand (which was apparently permanent enough to warrant presentation in our guide book!) for much needed nourishment and caught-up with the crew supporting their hockey buddy whom we had met in Orisson. Despite not wanting to continue, we had no choice as no accommodations were available for the next 6 km (about 4 miles). The last miles were grueling. We passed hay piled perhaps 50 feet in the air in tight rectangular packs. Jameson was so far ahead of me that I couldn't see him. I saw the French singing girls and played Bruce Springsteen's *Thunder Road* in my head repeatedly again using the lyrics as prayer. Finally, I entered Los Arcos, population 1200. I

Jameson on the long road to Los Arcos.

walked down the narrow central street looking for the church peak which signaled the city square and found Jordi, Robin and Frank drinking beer but no Jameson. And, no one had seen him! I panicked. Robin sensed my concern and jumped up telling me to walk one way down the main street and he would go the other way. I tried texting and calling his cell. My mind raced to the worst—that he was lost many miles away. Thankfully, just a couple minutes later I saw him with the hockey group using their cell phone to try to call me! I yelled and he turned. I hugged him and held him in joy that he was found. (Writing this, I realize this was just a taste of what Mary felt when she found Jesus in the temple.)

We tried to find accommodations. I went to hotels and albergues without finding anything. Robin and Jordi wanted to stay at the municipal albergue which had good reviews, but it was full. I had read about an albergue which was just down the road; they were able to accommodate us with 7 beds (3 bunkbeds and 1 single) in a room for 15 Euros. Jameson, Pablo, Frank, I, and another pilgrim stayed in that room. There was a large garden common area where we washed and dried clothes. The shared bathrooms were adequate. Robin and Jordi stayed in the room next to us (10 sets of bunkbeds but 5 Euros cheaper!) but regretted it due to snoring and other noise. I offered to pay the extra 5 Euros each for them, but they were too proud. I later learned that **Robin's stepfather** had forbid him to go and had seized his bank accounts leading to some financial concerns.

I was stressed as the next day was the longest hike yet, and we needed to complete it in order to catch the train to León. We headed back to town and, with an 8 pm pilgrim's Mass, dinner would have to be late. I was not happy. We shopped for gloves for Jameson who was getting sunburnt on his hands settling on a pair of cotton gloves from which I cut the fingertips. We walked into the church and I was not looking forward to another Mass in Spanish, understanding little to nothing. I went into the church hungry

The radiance of the altar in Los Arcos.

and not wanting to be there. Robin was going to join us as he always went with his grandfather to Mass on D-day but was nowhere to be seen. (Unbeknownst to us he had helped a Columbian man carry his backpack and they were treating him to dinner.) We walked into the church and elderly members of the community were saying the Rosary. We sat down, and I simmered. The priest walked in and turned on the lights—and WOW!—the altar radiated in the light. I got mad at myself for almost missing it. While Mass remained a struggle, the post-Mass pilgrim's blessing was beautiful. We had a nice pilgrim's meal just outside the church, and I hustled us to our room to sleep given the long day awaiting us the next day. We said our goodbyes to Robin, Jordi, and Frank knowing that we would likely not see them again. I hugged them all and said I loved them. We slept well.

The author's shadow on the Way.

Chapter 9

A train to catch in Logroño

The next day was rough—we knew it was going to be. We had 17 miles to hike and had to make it in one day or we'd miss the train to León. I set the alarm for 5:30 am and we left by 6 am. The temperature was in the 40's as we started—it was the only time I used my lightweight down coat other than as a pillow. We watched a beautiful sunrise and scared some sheep. (Jameson liked to joke he was king of the sheep!) I noticed at one point that we were walking between fields of wheat and vineyards (body and blood) and recalled my fascination with the miracle of turning water (rain) into wine via vineyards. We walked past a beautiful hexagonal church in Torres del Rio but it was locked given the early morning hour. I bought some provisions for lunch,

Sunrise leaving Los Arcos where we passed fields of grapes (wine) and wheat (bread).

and Jameson left his hiking gloves at a bus stop where we sat having a snack. This led to me going back for the gloves and Jameson beating himself up for the mistake—he was having a hard day. When I got the gloves, a bus bound for Logroño appeared. While tempting, we wanted to walk. We passed a mechanic's shop with a radio playing Bruce Springsteen's *Blinded by the Light* reminding us of how small the world was despite our physical distance from the United States.

After struggling through multiple Spanish Masses I wanted to participate in at least some way and decided that learning the Our Father in Spanish would be a start; then maybe the Hail Mary. Jameson and I were doing a Rosary most every day so I thought we could try it in Spanish. Jameson couldn't remember the Our Father in Spanish despite having memorized it in grade school, but then I met a fellow pilgrim from Arizona who was originally from Mexico. I asked him to speak it into my iPhone so I could repeat it. He gladly did and we engaged in conversation for a couple miles until we crested a little rise and were surprised by a substantial, impromptu memorial, consisting of about 100 yards of notes and mementos placed on rocks along the path. I reached down to see one which had a picture of two

Unexpected memorial of personal notes and mementos on the Way.

teenage boys on the front with the back reading something to the effect of "Your lives on earth were too short but we'll see you again. Love, mom and dad." I immediately began to cry and couldn't stop for about an hour thinking of the family's grief but also my own grief. My wife had suffered at least four recognized miscarriages, many of which were extremely difficult for her. They never really affected me that much because, as a man, I didn't feel the presence of the developing human life as she did. She likes to say that we have an angel watching over each of our four living children! I started grieving for our children that I never met and starting incorporating them into our Rosary at the end when we would pray for each member of our family (e.g., Saint Karyn, pray for us) by including them as Angelicus Uno, pray for us; Angelicus Dos, pray for us; Angelicus Tres, pray for us; Angelicus Cuatro, pray for us.

We stopped for a snack at a historic ruin and some Spanish ladies out for an afternoon walk wished us "Buen Apetito!" We came to Viana, a beautiful town, and stopped at a lovely café directly across from the Cathedral of Saint Maria and had a nice lunch although Jameson remained in a dour mood, and—with 9.4 km to go—I knew it was going to be a long haul. Before moving on, we went into the church to admire the beauty and get a stamp in our credentials. I noticed some prayer cards and asked the ladies who gave us the stamp if they had a prayer card for the Our Father in Spanish, Padre Nuestro. These women, easily in their 70's, told me in halting English to "Google it." (I eventually did...) The African American husband-wife couple from

Los Angeles came through town—the husband wanted to carry on and the wife wanted to stop and stay. They decided to travel separately. (We never heard how this turned out.) We toured the ruins of San Pedro and passed through the gate of Saint Francis into the countryside and out of town. Jameson's mood seemed to improve and we laughed and talked about many things.

Rotunda in Cathedral of Saint Maria in Viana.

The path took us through a park with campsites where trees provided very nice shade and then passed an industrial area, making us think we were getting closer to our destination. We went under a couple underpasses where several pilgrims were taking shelter from the mid-day heat, including the priest from Italy. We pressed on tired but motivated and literally between a rock and a hard place as the next significant accommodations were in Logroño. We walked down a long gravel road and passed a souvenir and stamp stand run by an old woman, Dona Feliza, who we found out was a Camino celebrity. She makes a living selling trinkets but also keeping a tally of how many pilgrims have passed on any given day—her manual tally on that day was over 300! I asked her how far to Logroño and, though not speaking any English, seemed to indicate that we were close.

We passed a city park and then crossed a bridge over río Ebro and into Logroño! We used my iPhone map to find the albergue, Pension La Bilbaina Logroño, which was award winning with a framed newspaper article (in Spanish) stating that they were carrying on an ancient tradition caring for pilgrims. The room was fantastic and we took a siesta. Upon awakening I got a text from Robin, Jordi, and Frank that they had taken a bus from Viana to Logroño to have one last dinner with us. And, they had friends—two young female physicians, Kate and Abby, from the United Kingdom. We had a lovely dinner and delightful ice cream cones after which we wisely said *adios* instead of heading out with them for tequila. But, this really was goodbye.

Our last dinner on the first leg of our pilgrimage. Clockwise from lower left: Jameson, Jordi, Abby, Kate, Pablo, Robin, Frank, the author.

Padre nuestro
que estás en los cielos,
santificado sea tu nombre,
venga tu reyno,
hagase tu voluntad,
asì en la tierra como en el cielo.
Danos hoy nuestro pan cotidiano,
y perdónanos nuestras deudas,
asì como nosotros perdonamos
    á nuestros deudores.
y no nos metas en tentación,
mas líbranos de mal.

Our Father,
who art in heaven,
hallowed be thy name,
thy kingdom come,
thy will be done,
on earth as it is in heaven.
Give us this day, our daily bread,
and forgive us our trespasses
as we forgive those who trespass
    against us.
And lead us not into temptation,
but deliver us from evil.

Chapter 10

The easy way to León

It was weird to sleep in—to 8 am! We got packed, left the lovely albergue, and had a quick breakfast in town. We walked to the city square, Plaza Mercado, and found the Cathedral, Santa María de la Redonda Cathedral, open and went inside. No charge, and beautiful. Perhaps the most noteworthy piece of art was an original by Miguel Ángel (better known as Michelangelo!) called the "Calvario" (the Calvary). For 50 cents the backlights dimmed, presumably to protect the picture, and the lights in the vault containing the painting turned on. We walked back out on the square and met a mother and young son of about 8 who had just finished their Camino—her husband was continuing but they had planned to only go this far. They were staying in Logroño for a festival the next day. We got some provisions (ibuprofen, snack bars, money from an

Michelangelo's *Calvario*.

ATM), and then walked to the train station. It was weird to use a mode of transportation other than walking but we quickly got used to the comfortable chairs. We had a short ride to a transfer city, Mirando de Ebro, where we had to wait for about 1.5 hours and got a bite to eat. The trip to León was uneventful. Getting off the train we headed towards our treat, the 5-star Parador hotel, but first passed the lesser known fountain of León (a drinking water fountain in a park!) and a beheaded cow statue. We crossed the Plaza San Marcs and took pictures in front of the impressive Parador with its spectacular façade containing many historic figures, one of which is faceless.

The Parador hotel chain was started in the early 1900's by a king of Spain, Alfonso XIII, to repurpose historic buildings (e.g. castles, fortresses, monasteries) and promote tourism. The hotels tend to be luxurious and encourage "heritage tourism." The Parador of León was made famous in the movie *The Way*. The building dates back to the 16th century and was the western headquarters for the Military Order of Saint James. In addition to the luxurious hotel, it houses a museum; we unfortunately arrived too late to tour. We checked in—nothing like taking a backpack to a 5-star hotel, but they are apparently used to it and offer pilgrims a steep discount—and checked into our BEAUTIFUL room! While tempting to lounge around the room, we were antsy to walk. We passed the real fountain of León and entered the city center where there was a celebration of the anniversary of the modern (post-Franco) Spanish Air Force. It was quite odd to see a modern fighter jet juxtaposed to Gaudi's neo-Gothic Casa Botines and the 16th Century Palacio de los Guzmanes, but, hey, Spain is a mix of old and new whirled together with lots of flair.

The luxurious Parador in León welcomes pilgrims for a brief respite on the Way.

We did an audio tour of the Cathedral, Pulchra Leonina, with its tall stained windows which let in beautiful colored light. We learned of the precarious renovations of this 13th century construction from the 15th century until the 19th century to repair a suboptimal foundation built on Roman ruins. Perhaps most interesting to us was the introduction of the pregnant Virgin Mary in statues including a side chapel in León's Cathedral. To an American who has never seen Mary depicted in this state, it was odd at first but then made so much sense—the very pregnant Mary

Pregnant Mother Mary statue.

representing hope in the birth of Christ who would transform this world. After spending about an hour touring just before closing, we exited into the Plaza Regia to find a crowd watching a dog obstacle course—another Spanish paradox with this sideshow in the shadow of the magnificent Cathedral towering just behind them! We found a nice restaurant and had great conversation over dinner—conversations with Jameson were a highlight the entire trip. We shared things that both of us probably would not have shared in other settings. Walking back to the luxurious Parador, we stopped for ice cream (and a cookie on top!). Before settling in for the night I checked how many miles we walked—about 7 miles—not bad for a day taking a train!

Outside the Cathedral in León.

Inside the Cathedral in León.

Chapter 11

A close call with vegetarians in Hospital de Órbigo

We got up early the next morning and had an extraordinary buffet among well attired tourists who commented on the fascinating pilgrims as if we weren't even present! How much I wanted to tell them I was a well-respected and accomplished ENT surgeon from the United States who had chosen to do this of my own free will to strengthen my spiritual side, but I held back. We checked out and called a taxi cab to bypass the very industrious part of León (just like the train, it felt very weird using transportation other than walking!). And I—using my point and repeat mode of Spanish communication—asked the taxi

Opción outside León where we rejoined the Way.

cab to take us to *opción* just past the airport, not realizing until later that I was asking him to take us to an "optional" branch point of the trail! Somehow we got to the correct point and started walking again, at which point both Jameson and I felt like we were intruding because we had skipped over a large portion of the trail and now we were going to be "intruding" into the Camino of others who may have walked the entire way. Luckily, this quickly passed as we reminded ourselves that many others were doing the Way in sections and some were even starting from León or further on.

Trail maker (yellow arrow and shell) pointing us along the second half of our pilgrimage.

It felt good to be walking again. But then it got hot and we realized today's trek was going to be long, straight, and relatively boring—the kind of day where a tree in the distance doesn't change much for hours and your mind plays tricks on you about the reasons you are doing the Camino despite repetitive prayers to chase away those negative thoughts. We stopped at various towns to get food, drink, and/or apply blister protection tape (should have bought stock in Compeed!) and met various pilgrims, including a Floridian who seemed more like a Texan. He told us, after an incredibly long, straight, hot, boring walk that "It wasn't but a thing." That saying became a recurring theme to cheer ourselves up, and we kept running into Tex (we never got his first name), who turned out to be a very interesting, nice man who was hiking the whole Camino sharing parts with his adult son and adult daughter.

Long Roman bridge leading into Hospital de Órbigo.

We rallied to get to Hospital de Órbigo—an ambitious goal of over 16 miles for the day, but we had spent the night at the Parador and felt it was the right day to push. We were so exhausted upon arrival at Hospital de Órbigo that we barely appreciated the beautiful long Roman bridge and jousting fields that are still used in festivals today. We meandered around town looking for Casa Verde which had been recommended by our parish priest as a vegetarian, yoga hostel that "somehow worked." We had a clerk from the Parador call and arrange the reservation and had high hopes. I should have remembered that the key to happiness is to have low expectations and then have them exceeded!

We had a hard time finding Casa Verde but finally—after seemingly completely walking around the town—we arrived. The house had a beautiful yard and garden and we went up to the second floor where the kitchen and common area were located to check-in and pay. They were preparing a vegetarian dinner and asked if we had any dietary restrictions. We were shown our room on the first floor which had a double bed that pretty much took up the entirety of the room! There were two bathrooms that were shared with another room which had three or four sets of bunk beds. We showered and arranged for our wash to be done and sat out in the beautiful yard to catch up on journaling and play cribbage. Then, we were invited to participate in a yoga class in their yoga room; Jameson quickly said yes although he could tell I had reservations. We made our way to the yoga room—a large room with a heater in it even though it was about 90 degrees outside—and were invited to "introduce yourself to the room" by walking around and touching the walls, mats, and—in a polite fashion—the other participants. Over a period of 30-45 minutes we were asked to assume various poses and stretches, some of which felt good. As Jameson noted on his blog, I was clearly outside of my comfort zone, but he was glad I had at least tried it. After the yoga we went upstairs to try and arrange accommodations for the next couple days asking the proprietor to call ahead to future towns for us.

Next came dinner—a lovely affair outside under the setting sun consisting of salad, soy milk, vegetarian pizza, baba ghanoush (mashed eggplant), and vegan bread (no butter). Overall, okay, but our bodies were craving animal protein. After dinner, a song about being thankful was performed, and we were invited to stay for an extra day—worldwide yoga day—the following day. We politely declined and got ready for bed after spending some time talking with a German woman who had suffered an orthopedic injury the year before when she tried to complete the Camino and was laid up at Casa Verde for 3 weeks or so; she had returned this year to try again. She was hiking with her dog and sleeping in a small single tent which she had placed at the side of Casa Verde. She felt very much in tune with Casa Verde and was very nice to Jameson and me. After watching a beautiful sunset (sunset is late in Spain in summer) we made way to our "double room" and got some sleep.

Sunset at vegetarian albergue in Hospital de Órbigo.

Chapter 12
Astorga, my kind of town

We got up the next morning early and were the first to leave. We were on a mission—a mission to find *carne*! We quickly found a café on the outskirts of town and had some eggs and ham and met some inhabitants who looked like they were just coming home from the preceding Friday night's celebrations and some teens who looked as if they had camped out overnight. We passed a crew cleaning up a festival at Santibáñez de Valdeiglesia—perhaps where the late night revelers were coming from! We passed a graffiti'd sign that was barely visible but read "Cheer Up," at a time

Unexpected encouraging signs abound on the Camino.

when I needed it most. Next up was a free refreshment stand, la Casa de los Dioses Cantina, where the proprietor, David, was offering fruit and other treats for whatever payment you were willing to offer even if that was nothing. It was amazing that so many people were encouraging pilgrims! We were a little worn from the vegetarian casa, and I wanted to try a hotel. (Jamis was not in disagreement this time!) I called a hotel in Astorga from a billboard advertisement, and we got the last room available that night.

We came to a stone cross, Cruceiro Santo Toribio, commemorating a 5th century bishop, which overlooks the suburbs and then the city of Astorga. The city rests on a small crest with mountains, the Montes de León, beyond the city limits. Within these mountains lay the Cruz de Ferro, the highest point of the Camino. A busker was singing and aggressively seeking donations and became almost indignant when we did not contribute (we didn't even stop but by just walking by he felt he deserved some payment— a recurring theme we would encounter). We passed by a clever pilgrim fountain that, when activated to fill your water bottle, would also have water come out of a gourd to the mouth of the pilgrim in the statue.

We hiked through suburbs of Astorga and then an industrial section where we crossed over a railroad track via a pedestrian walkway that was huge and out of proportion to what was needed to cross the tracks being over-engineered (from an engineer's perspective!). We hiked up a steep bluff and entered the old town of Astorga passing the municipal

Cruceiro Santo Toribio with Astorga in the midground and the Montes de León in the background.

albergue and one of several churches in town. We poked our heads in and it appeared a funeral was occurring. Roman ruins were visible below Plexiglas windows. We overlooked río Jerga and tried to buy food from a stand in a park, but it was too early and they weren't serving yet. We found our hotel and checked in and showered. It was just what we needed. Of the hotels we stayed in, it was among our top three (with only those top three having AC!). We got hamburgers at a restaurant next door which was quite busy because it was Saturday and fans of soccer were gathering. We had a siesta with AC and then rallied to tour Astorga. This was tough as Jameson was dragging, but boy were we glad we did!

We started at Gaudi's Bishop's Palace, originally built to house the Bishop of Astorga when Astorga used to be an important town where three ancient trade routes

Jameson in front of Gaudi's Bishop's Palace in Astorga.

crossed. Now, it functions as a museum. I was fascinated with the architecture of the building (the basement contains an unusual "long arch," the only time it was used in a Gaudi building) and an incredibly beautiful chapel. Jameson was more captivated by the artwork displayed including progressive representations of the human form from abstract to realistic including Saint Agatha holding her amputated breasts. We then went over to the adjacent Astorga Cathedral with its huge vaulted ceiling which was Jameson's favorite to this point (it would be displaced by the Cathedral in Santiago). We got out just before closing time and headed back to the plaza outside our hotel for a pilgrim's meal to watch the giant animated clock at the top of the hour. It was the eve of Trinity Sunday and we forewent desert

Chapel within the Bishop's Palace.

to get to vigil Mass at Saint Bartholomew's where three priests concelebrated (appropriate for Trinity Sunday!), and we saw the dramatic Mary of the Seven Sorrows. We went back to the restaurant for our desert and then headed to bed knowing we had a couple of the most grueling hiking days just ahead of us.

Mary's seven sorrows at Saint Bartholomew's in Astorga.

Grand entrance of the Cathedral in Astorga.

Gilded main altar within Cathedral in Astorga

Chapter 13

Rabanal – is that all you have?

Awaking early, we got breakfast at the hotel with a group doing the Camino for diabetes awareness including some with artificial limbs. They had support cars and their bags were being ported ahead. I became concerned that the Way would become more and more crowded with such groups but quickly realized that the Way is long with lots of wide open areas. My concerns were unfounded! After this realization, I felt embarrassed that I was concerned about sharing the Way with people who had clearly suffered more than I had. We passed the albergue in Las Águedas which was a school house converted into an albergue. I remember looking in and feeling both gratitude that we had stayed in a hotel in Astorga but also regret that we did not share the experience with other pilgrims. At about the halfway point to our intended destination of Rabanal, we came across the famous Cowboy Bar in El Ganso and had a sustaining lunch.

We continued to Via Cucis, just outside of Puente de Pañote, where sticks were woven into the wire mesh fence in the shape of crosses—I added one of my own. We made it to Rabanal earlier than expected. Both Jameson and I felt good at this point and, after ensuring that our lodging in Foncebadón was secure (the yoga albergue we had secured from Casa Verde did not have a room but "guaranteed" that we would have a room at the nearby hotel), we forfeited our room in Rabanal and headed up the steep 5 km (200 m of rise) to Foncebadón. We were in good spirits and laughing. The climb was grueling but the vistas beautiful. We had reached our halfway point—150 miles in!—and felt pretty good. Perhaps we were going to make it.

Jameson at the famous Cowboy Bar. (He used this as his picture for his college freshmen directory.)

My contribution to the "cross" fence.

We came into Foncebadón expecting a bigger town but found a very rustic mountain top villa with only 10 or 12 structures. We said "hi" to the proprietor at the yoga albergue, were directed to the nearby hotel, and invited to return to have vegetarian paella for dinner (Jameson asked if we could add meat to it!). We politely declined. The hotel was okay, with two beds and a private bath in a loft room where I hit my head on the ceiling repeatedly. We showered, did laundry, and then had dinner where we met a British artist who had previously hiked the Camino but was now car camping painting at various points. He seemed more interested in our company than we in his, but we obliged his request and joined him for dinner and had good conversation during which he showed us some of his works.

Knowing that we had another 100 m climb over 2 km the next morning to reach the highest point of the Camino where an iron cross marked the pinnacle, we retired for the evening. Our window was open, and despite being at high altitude (about 4500 feet above sea level) the temperature was still elevated. Guitar music from the yoga albergue wafted in. Sleep came slowly.

Just outside Foncebadón near the highest elevation of the Camino.

Chapter 14

Cruz de Ferro – the peak, or not...

We rose early as was our habit. The general store opened at 6:30 am, and we got some hard boiled eggs, oranges, and breakfast bars. The hike up was tough, but we were motivated—this was the peak where we would leave our small pebbles brought from Tennessee signifying our shedding of issues/problems. We arrived just about sunrise and found the cross as described in the guidebook as a "humble marker." We saw the painter with whom we had dinner the night before; he was setting up his easel and said "hello." The Camino police—sort of like Park Rangers—were questioning him. He told us they were concerned because someone had tried to set fire to the telephone pole on the top of which the iron cross was affixed. We climbed the stone mound and left our pebbles. We took pictures and felt comforted that we had achieved this mark. We pressed on for the mammoth 800 m descent over the next 20 km. It did not go as planned.

Shortly after summiting, Jameson developed a nosebleed which I was able to control with Afrin. We soldiered on. The descent was difficult and rocky. Jameson was getting ahead of me and fearful of losing him as I had in Los Arcos (and without support from our "GodSpell" posse!), I hurried down the trail, leading to development of blisters. We passed through the mountain town of Acebo and stopped in the small chapel. We made sandwiches from supplies we had bought in Foncebadón. Just outside of

Summiting at Cruz de Ferro and leaving our stones.

Acebo, we passed a large hotel with an inviting pool where the diabetes group was staying. We continued our descent on the road and then onto rocky paths with steeper and steeper descents and Jameson farther and farther ahead of me. I was recognizing some fellow *peregrinos* (Spanish for pilgrims) from the days before, but we had yet to make connections as we had with Frank, Jordi, and Robin, and I was concerned about getting separated from my son. I again hurried exacerbating blisters that were developing.

I finally caught Jameson and told him to slow down. He did not look good. I encouraged him to drink water. We made it to Molinaseca, a beautiful village of only 800 which appeared to be a weekend getaway on the beautiful río Meruelo, but we had intended to make it to Ponferrada, a much larger town of some 70,000. We stopped for some food outside a grocery store. Jameson felt clammy and would not take off his safari shirt even though the temperature was in

The refreshing río Meruelo in Molinaseca.

the upper 80's. He told me he was cold. I knew we couldn't continue and went back into the grocery store to ask the proprietor, who spoke almost no English, about a room. He somehow understood and indicated that there was a room directly above the grocery and showed it to me. It was beautiful! I got Jameson. He showered, and then took a siesta in AC. After a long nap, he felt much better, and we explored this lovely town where I hope to return someday. We went to the river and watched people swimming. We toured the local church and then got dinner and watched children playing in the streets which made me miss our youngest son, Zachary. We knew we were a bit behind and had to make up time, but I was just glad that Jameson was feeling better and that we had safe haven for the night.

Children playing in Molinaseca reminded me of our youngest son Zachary causing me to miss him terribly.

Chapter 15

Do you know the way through Ponferrada?

We woke refreshed and headed out with a couple provisions to tide us over until we hit a spot for breakfast. We saw a few pilgrims, including a woman who appeared to be in a disagreement with her husband, but we later realized that her husband was supporting her Camino by bringing supplies at various stops. After a Rosary and great discussion, we entered the old city of Ponferrada and had breakfast directly across from the Castillo de los Templarios—a 12th century Templar Castle. We walked through the old town and the Way became difficult to follow through the city. We stopped at a pharmacy for some more Compeed (blister bandages) and asked if we were on the right path. We were told, yes, the Camino de Santiago is this way.

12th century Templar castle in Ponferrada.

While most of the people in this busy city of 70,000 people essentially ignored us, an older man greeted us with "Buen Camino" and assured us we were on the right path when we came across a round-about with five choices. We continued to walk, and the Way became much more industrial. The sky started to look very ominous with dark clouds and lightning visible in the distance. We stopped in a grocery store to buy some fruit. A very nice woman let me go ahead of her because I only had two oranges—the cashier assured us we were on the Camino de Santiago. We came across a hardware store and, again without speaking any Spanish and without them speaking any English, was able to buy extra bumpers for our walking poles to use in urban areas—the cashier assured us we were on the Camino de Santiago. But, we were growing skeptical because we continued to be in a very urban area. We stopped at an underpass of a highway and realized that we had missed a turn-off for the main Camino trail and were on a four lane road literally called the Camino de Santiago!

However, all was not lost—the road was actually a shortcut and would join up with the main Camino a mile or two down the road. Jameson expressed doubts, but I took the approach of *felix culpa*, O Happy Fault, a theological concept that boils down to "make lemonade out of lemons" based on the fault, Christ's passion, that resulted in the gift, opening of heaven. After a couple more blocks the sky looked even worse, and we stopped in someone's driveway to put on our rain gear. An elderly Spanish lady came out of the house and we thought she would either shoo us away or provide shelter from the impending storm, but she just greeted us "Buen Camino" and through her expressions let us know that we were going the right way. We carried on and then the heavens opened up and it poured with thunder and lightning, albeit lasting only about 15-20 minutes—but they were a terrifying 15-20 minutes and all I could think about was coming this far only to be struck dead by lightning! After the rain stopped, I went into a café (soaking wet and dripping on their floor!) and asked if we were on the right path—we were assured that we were. A couple miles down the road I saw a café advertising a pilgrim's meal and knew we were soon to reunite with the main Camino!

We stopped in the café and found other pilgrims (we hadn't seen any since Ponferrada!) and ordered some Aquarius (essentially Gatorade) and used the restroom. A bagpipe school—we were very close to the Galicia region of Spain—was just behind the café and the music, presumably by the students, was not very good. Jameson, already in a bad mood, was soured even worse by the music and the realization that his water-proof raincoat was still not water-proof! We carried on over a major highway and into rural areas, which was much appreciated after hiking through the industrial areas. Jameson was pretty down on himself—I tried to cheer him up but he needed to work through it himself. Thank God neither of us was down at the same time during our journey. (That is, until the very last day!) We passed a closed mobile café that had picnic tables and decided to take off our raingear. My blisters from the descent from the Cruz de Ferro were irritating me more and more and I adjusted the lacing of my boots. There was another pilgrim there doing the same thing and I glanced at his feet—he was hiking in sport sandals and I couldn't believe the horrible state of his feet which were almost completely covered in blisters with pus coming from under his toenails. I felt ashamed complaining about my little blisters.

Because of our "shortcut" (*felix culpa!*), we had only a couple more miles to reach Cacabelos where I had made a reservation at a hotel. Jameson didn't want to stay at another hotel, but he desperately needed a bathroom and acquiesced when we got there. After cleaning up, we toured the town and got a gyro at a market that was just about to close for siesta. We played cribbage in the indoor market while the rain drizzled onto the metal roof. We toured the local church—it had a little plaque celebrating its 900th anniversary in 2008 ("Isn't but a thing!") but didn't have a Mass that night. We got dinner and bought Jameson some biking gloves to protect his hands from the sun. After some more cribbage we went to bed early realizing that, because of the last couple day's shortened hikes, we really needed to make up some distance if we were to make Santiago on schedule—and with a flight to Paris for a medical conference looming, we had to make it on time, even if that meant taking a taxi or a bus which we did not want to do.

Jameson with Saint James statue in front of Hotel Villa de Cacabelos.

Crucifix outside 910 year old church.

Chapter 16
The long, uphill road to Ruitelán

Getting an early start, we had a nice breakfast and headed out of town, passing the municipal albergue which looked unique, with small individual "pods" consisting of a chalet with two beds centered about a common area. We crossed the río Cúa and began an uphill hike. We passed another vegetarian albergue (how close we came to staying in a string of such albergues!). We came to an *opción* (I now knew what it meant!) and chose the more rural path through Valtuille and then came to Villafranca, a charming town dating back to the Middle Ages which had a beautiful church (every town had a beautiful church!) and cut-back narrow streets that reminded me of *National Lampoon's European*

Switchback road in Villafranca.

Vacation. After stopping for a snack, we pressed on, crossing the río Burbia. My blisters were causing me much discomfort with a stabbing pain in my heels with each step I took. I sincerely did not know if I could go on. But, in reality, there were not a lot of options. To stop at this point would mean finding a ride back to Ponferrada and then taking a train to a bigger city to fly to either Santiago or Paris and then home. I kept walking. Surprisingly, after a couple miles the blister areas went numb.

The guidebook said there were two paths from Villafranca, at 500 m, to O'Cebreiro, at 1300 m—either a very steep and demanding path or a less demanding path which suffered from following a busy road. After we completed our Camino, both Jameson and I read the book *I'm Off Then,* by Hape Kerkaling (the book from which Frank was telling us stories), who hiked the Camino in 2001 prior to the building of the bypass highway which dramatically reduced the traffic. Hape notes that this was perhaps the worst part of the Camino for him and his traveling companions, and he often felt his life was on the line due to the traffic. The incline was intense as was the heat. The only inkling we had of what awaited us was a scribble in our guidebook from our parish priest which read "long day." The hike took us through the Valcare Valley along the río Pereje. There were moments of beauty juxtaposed with cars barreling down the twisting highway at very high rates of speed only feet away from us. Our guidebook recommended that pilgrims hum with increasing intensity as a car or truck approached and then fade the intensity as the vehicle moved on to counteract the noxious sound of the engine. While some people might find that helpful, we didn't. At every option (or *opción!*), we would take side roads to bypass the highway for brief respites from the traffic.

We stopped and had lunch at a café in Crispeta. This café appeared to be a stop for every pilgrim as there were so few places to stop and eat. Jameson and I still felt like outsiders on our second half of the Camino because we had yet to bond with fellow pilgrims as we had with Frank, Jordi, and Robin. We hiked through the town of Trabedelo and then took a break at what appeared to be a highway rest stop where the A-6 crossed the smaller N-VI which was the road we were hiking near. Large transport trucks were coming off the interchange as we sat on a large rock and ate our snack. It was very hot and we were not sure how much longer it would take to arrive at the rural hotel where I had secured for the night in Ruitelán. We passed by a lovely albergue just outside of Vega de Valcarce which offered pilgrims access to the nearby river and were envious of the sojourners enjoying the river. We forced ourselves to have lunch at a small café just before it closed for siesta—another ham and cheese *bocadillo*. We pressed on and passed an ironically positioned sign that warned of snow which we couldn't imagine in the June heat.

Snow? Really?!?

I kept checking my iPhone for distances, encouraging Jameson—"only a mile or two to go!" But, I was discouraged. And then suddenly we came upon our lodging for the night—a beautiful hotel called El Paraíso del Bierzo, which was literally in the middle of nowhere. We checked in and, after cleaning up, asked the clerk to call ahead and make a reservation for the next night. We found out that this rural hotel was run by a family and had award winning food. We came down for dinner and realized that we were a bit out of place being surrounded by older affluent people, including a couple who appeared to be on their honeymoon! Being hungry and with no other restaurants nearby, we greedily ate everything brought to the table.

Towards the end of the meal, we noticed a group of four older ladies staring off intently, concentrating on the field below us. We politely asked what was happening and one said she believed a cow was giving birth. This captivated many of us, especially how the owner of the hotel, who also owned the field and livestock, did not intervene but rather let nature take its course. The older ladies were from Australia and included one who was a farmer. She told us how different this was from the United States or Australia where the farmer would have a vet present concerned that the calf or mother might not survive. We watched for a couple of hours as the calf came into the world, got to his or her feet, and started nursing. Amazed by the life force inherent within us all, we found new motivation for the next day's journey, which would be another doozy—thank God we didn't realize it that night as we might have had restless sleep!

Chapter 17
*O'Cebreiro, the places you'll go
and the people you'll meet*

We thought we had our hardest days behind us, but we soon realized we were wrong. (Sound like a recurring theme?) We were facing a 700 m rise to a peak of 1300 m in just over 7 km. The morning started off brisk, and we felt great. The rise soon became rather steep but the views, which

Sharing the beautiful view with a bull (fence not shown!).

we shared with a bull, were worth it! We reached the top and had a small snack on a stone wall which allowed unfettered views of the vista (no bull!). We toured Iglesia de Santa Maria Real, a church dating back to the 9th century, and, according to our guide book, the oldest church associated with the Camino and the site of a miracle where a humble peasant witnessed the wine and bread of Eucharist turn into the body and blood of Christ in front of a haughty priest. We walked inside the church and came upon an amazing display of Bibles from various languages (including braille!) opened to the readings for the day. We got our credentials stamped and ambled into the small town just beyond, where school field trips were occurring. We found a restaurant and got a large breakfast. When I went to use the restroom, I saw out the window that the clouds were rolling into the valley below, creating unbelievably beautiful views.

The exterior of Iglesia de Santa Maria Real in O'Cebreiro (left) and inside (right) where Bibles from many languages are opened to the readings of the day.

Out of the corner of my eye I spied a woman falling asleep sitting at a table. We pressed on passing into the Galacia region of Spain—the final region we would hike through—and contended with bicyclists racing down the

Clouds filling the valley below O'Cebreiro.

curvy switchback roads. Very unexpectedly, I had to use the restroom, but again the Camion provided—a café with a lovely bathroom appeared out of nowhere! As we moved on, we passed a non-descript old church (while beautiful, there were so many beautiful churches that we were becoming immune) with a bell tower on which a couple teenage girls were climbing. They asked us if we were American, and I said we were. They—parents Robin and Julie, both physicians from Seattle, and their 15 and 13 year old daughters, Jane and Kat—had started the Camino just three days prior in Ponferrada. And, that woman falling asleep in O'Cebreiro, was Jane!

We walked and talked for hours which was just what Jameson needed to push ahead. Just ahead of them was a family friend, Eric, an emergency room doctor from Seattle, who had arrived a bit late but caught up to them. Little did we know we had just found our second "Godspell" posse with whom we would finish our pilgrimage! During this time we learned a lot about each other. Jane and Kat had finished school the day before they left. Eric, their dear family friend, had decided on the spur of the moment to join them but got delayed in Chicago with a soon-to-be expired passport.

Somehow he got it resolved and, after extensive travel, literally waltzed into a café outside Ponferrada which just happened to be the exact spot where Julie, Robin, Jane and Kat were having breakfast! (Camino magic! Sound like a recurring theme?) After walking with the Seattle crew for a couple of hours, they stopped for lunch while we pressed on uncertain that we would see them again. We crested at the pilgrim statue at Alto do Poio and took a picture at the famous statue.

We were only about half way to our destination of Triacastela but felt good meeting the Seattle group and knowing that the rest of today's hike was downhill. During this descent we passed a quarry where ancient pilgrims would pick up stones to be used in the Cathedral at Santiago—we could not imagine adding stones to our packs at this point! We walked through the small village of Filloval tiptoeing around livestock dung and bought some raspberries that were left on a table with a suggested donation of one Euro. Between Filloval and Triacastela the path reminded us of

Jameson re-enacting the pilgrim state at Alto do Poio.

scenes from *The Hobbit*, with trees arching over the sunken path. The shade was sooooo appreciated! I kept checking my iPhone—17 miles, 18 miles—when was it going to end? And then, suddenly, we exited "The Shire" and stepped onto the beginning of an asphalt road which marked the edge of the 900 person village of Triacastela. We had made it—20 miles!—our longest hike of the Camino! We had used an online booking service to reserve a room at Casa García which provided very adequate accommodations and satisfying pilgrim's meals. Following the pilgrim's guide, we went to 6 pm Mass with Fr. Augusto, all in Spanish, of which I understood nothing until his pilgrim's blessing in English. The church was packed and had a unique front with three stones commemorating the three castles which used to stand in this town. After another meal—we just couldn't seem to get enough calories into our bodies—we were off to bed despite the sky still showing signs of day. It didn't matter—after 20 miles we slept soundly.

The church in Triacastela where Fr. Augusto blessed pilgrims in English.

Chapter 18

Sarria: where many join the Way

We awoke late (if you call 8 am late!) because we only had 12 miles to hike and treated ourselves to a nice breakfast. Most of the hike was through lovely forest. Jameson and I spent a lot of time alone with our thoughts. My mind filled with thoughts of guardian angels—why did I not feel mine so strongly—I thought of names and settled on the reverse of my name of Robert, Trebor. I asked God to tell me what he wanted me to do with the years I have left on this earth. The answer didn't come as a burning bush or the

Jameson hiking towards Sarria.

wind, but the knowledge that what I was doing was exactly what God wanted me to do spread over me. I reflected on the prayer of Saint Theresa, which was read by the salutatorian at Jameson's graduation.

> *May today there be peace within.*
> *May you trust God that you are exactly where you are meant to be.*
> *May you not forget the infinite possibilities that are born of faith.*
> *May you use those gifts that you have received, and pass on the love that has been given to you.*
> *May you be content knowing that you are a child of God.*
> *Let this presence settle into your bones, and allow your soul the freedom to sing, dance, praise, and love.*
> *It is there for each and every one of us.*

But then I also reflected on Fr. Joe McMahon's greatest fear—that he makes it to the pearly gates and Saint Peter asks him "Joe, why didn't you enjoy it more?"

The hike was through lovely forests with plenty of shade and beautiful weather. We passed the Our Lady of the Snows scallop fountain. We stopped at a great café in Furela —Casa do Franco—where the proprietor had done the Camino and catered to pilgrims in a way only a fellow pilgrim could understand. We left a coin on the mantle and carried on. In short time we got to Sarria passing a park on the outskirts and then stopping at a hiking supply store to buy more bumpers for our walking sticks. We found our hotel, and it had AC! We showered, siesta'd, and went out to explore.

To enter the old city, one has to hike up about 100 stairs—Jameson started humming the *Rocky* theme song! We had dinner in a diner where the proprietor was maître d, bartender, short order cook, and town gossip—all at the same time. Boy, did I wish that I understood Spanish! We went to a 20 minute Mass in a centuries old church where the priest pulled up to the front door in his old Honda at the last minute and gave us a final blessing in English. And, I got a 20 minute open blade shave by an elderly Spanish barber just moments after telling Jameson that if we saw a barber I needed to stop. I briefly realized in the midst of the shave that a man who

Our Lady of the Snows fountain and reflecting pool.

spoke no English had an open blade against my neck and I spoke no Spanish. Somehow I let the thought pass and thoroughly enjoyed the process. Afterward, I asked how much I owed him—he said 3 Euros. I gave him 5 Euros, but he resisted. I insisted. Somehow we were able to communicate all this without a common spoken language.

Walking back to our hotel, we ran into Eric and Robin from Seattle and shared stories from the day and make plans for the next couple days. I stopped at a local grocery store and got provisions literally minutes before it closed and then stopped to get money out of an ATM. While we had another relatively short day ahead tomorrow—the guidebook listed it as 14 miles—we knew it was going to be unseasonably hot and headed to bed early so we could get an early start.

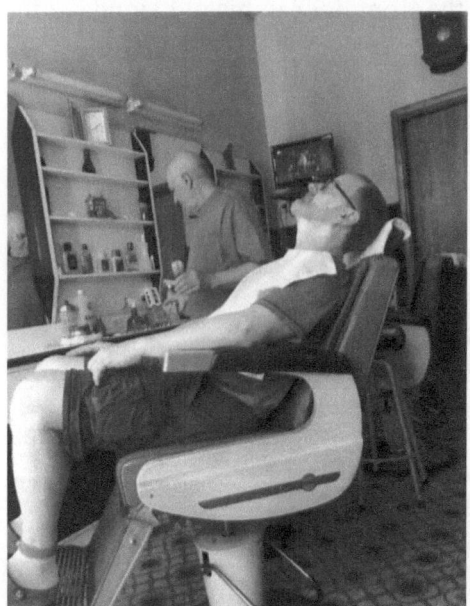

The author getting a shave from the barber of ~~Seville~~ Sarria.

Chapter 19

Portomarin: a city moved to make way for the Way

As planned, we got up and headed out before the sun rose. We re-climbed the 100 stairs (or more) to the old city. It was a misty morning. The Way was more crowded because this was the last town at which one could start and still get a certificate of completion for hiking 100 km. After we got out of town, the Way weaved through beautiful country side. About 5 km in, we passed an albergue where a group of students had stayed on their first night doing a field trip of the last 100 km. Our attention was disrupted. I was angry about the interruption, but quickly realized that they had as much of a right to do this pilgrimage as I did. This realization was hard because they played loud music from their cell phones and hiked at erratic paces. We engaged some of them who instead of wishing us "Buen Camino!" wished us the English translation—"Good Way!"—following which they giggled. I found out they were 7th graders, and we talked about Spanish and American culture, especially music.

We crossed by some high-end, ultra-modern houses that appeared to be out of place. I had wondered numerous times why the Way had not been commercialized beyond the rural stops that existed. Seeing what could happen made me hope that the trend would not continue. We stopped for breakfast at a café that was overwhelmed by the field trip crew. We passed a fellow pilgrim wearing a shirt from a high school near our home in Nashville. The pilgrim, Gordon, had gone to his first two years of high school there before his family relocated to Louisville. We talked about common friends and laughed at the coincidence. He was doing his second Camino, having done portions of it two years ago with his parents and younger sister who were with him on the trip. He talked about his experience this time—the first third of the trip was physically exhausting, the second third (through the high elevation Meseta) was emotionally exhausting hiking for days through landscape that changed little from day to day (reinforcing to us that we made the right decision to skip the Meseta!), and the final third was the true Camino where he finally felt that he was undergoing the transformation he sought. Interestingly, he wore sports sandals because his feet had blistered.

We approached Portomarin after a brief hike of only 14 miles. The original city of Portomarin was relocated high up on a hill in the early 1960's so that the Balesar reservoir could be built. No telling how many remains of pilgrims lay submerged under the reservoir. We crossed the bridge and up the steep staircase to the city. We were failing to appreciate how such steps could be welcoming! The casa rural that we were staying at, Casa Perez, was even farther up a hill! We passed a community center where bagpipe lessons were taking place—Jameson and I laughed about how much this had bothered him just days before. We checked in—no AC—but a fantastic shower with in-wall water jets almost made up for it. My ankles were hurting and Jameson's gastrointestinal track was acting up. As close as we were—only 4 more days of hiking—I still had doubts that we would make it.

We had a satisfying late lunch at the main house of Casa Perez (I had the octopus which was a local specialty) and, talking with the host and waiter, found that this Casa, like so many others, was a multi-generational, family-run business. When the door to the kitchen would open I could spy an elderly woman cooking on an elaborate stove that looked like it was from the 1950's! After a siesta hastened by our full stomachs, we went to town to explore the unique

The author at the top of the stairs to the relocated city of Portomarin with the Balesar reservoir in the background.

church which was relocated in 1962 from its original location (now submerged) and which appeared to be a single square bastion of a castle. The 7th grade field trip crew was playing soccer in the town square. We sat down for dinner, and Eric from Seattle appeared and asked to join us. As had occurred with earlier pilgrims, the conversation quickly turned deep. He told us his story. Eric was a burned-out emergency room doctor in Seattle who took a financial risk on building a large B&B which was finally paying off. In the fall, he would start his conversion to Catholicism via the Rite of Christian Initiation of Adults (RCIA) after not having much religion as a child growing up the son of an atheist urologist. We told him our stories. He and Jameson hit it off and, when Jameson had to go spend considerable time in the WC (a.k.a. bathroom), Eric told me how special he could sense Jameson was. When Jameson came back from the bathroom, Eric offered him a job in Seattle when we got back to the States! He didn't specify what he wanted Jameson to do other than model spirituality for his kids.

We went to the 8 pm pilgrims' Mass—again all in Spanish—*oy, vey*! We meet some other pilgrims Eric had befriended on the Way but, wanting to get an early start the next day given the continuing heat, we called it an early night. Eric asked if he could join us in the morning and we set a meeting time of 6:30 am. Both Jameson and I took cold showers before retiring in the hopes of cooling our bodies down so that we could sleep. It was somewhat successful.

Chapter 20
Palas de Rei where the blind see

Eric showed up right on time and we shared what little food we had—an orange and a couple breakfast bars. We hiked out of town crossing the outflow track of the reservoir. Eric had portaged his backpack ahead to the next town—a car would pick up his backpack and drop it off at the next stop, so he needed to carry only a day pack. We walked and talked about so many things—politics, the state of health care, our shared Catholic faith, raising kids—and stopped for brunch in Gonzar at Café Descanso del Peregrino where we had delicious melons wrapped in a variation of thin ham. They had customer service down to a science and easily handled the large pilgrim traffic.

Re-energized, we moved on another 5 km and stopped at the tiny chapel in Ventas de Narón where a large group of pilgrims got refreshments from a nearby café. I wandered over to the chapel which was locked, and, being the ignorant American, pulled a rope that was affixed to the side of the front door which rang a bell. I didn't think anything would happen but then an elderly, blind man appeared from the village using a white stick to navigate a path he clearly had taken many, many times. He opened the door to the chapel and went to a table near the front where he set up shop stamping credentials but with a twist. Because he could not see, he inked the auto-inking stamp and raised his hand at which point a pilgrim would guide his hand to the spot where they wanted the stamp and he would push down creating the stamp! We got our stamp and came outside to discover that Julie, Robin, Jane, and Kat had caught up with us. Eric bought popsicles for us all, and Jameson had another nosebleed! With the nosebleed controlled, we pushed on with the nucleus of the group with whom we would finish the Camino.

Jameson ringing the bell (left) notifying the blind attendant to come and stamp our credentials (right).

Time passed quickly as we talked amongst ourselves. I shared my story—academic ENT MD disenchanted with current employment yet at the same time so appreciative of the opportunities I had been given. Julie shared hers—academic psychiatrist who had suffered a series of unfortunate professional events. She had trained at the same place she was hired on-staff negating the effectiveness of her start-up package which delayed her tenure application because she was assigned so many other responsibilities including overseeing resident education. She had been forced to sign a non-compete clause but was promised it would not be enforced. Eventually, she couldn't take it anymore and left for private practice where she was thriving, but she was now having to deal with the non-compete clause. She did so trying to change the law in Washington State regarding non-compete clauses. She was a recent RCIA convert and was praying for her husband, Robin, whom she described as a "Jesuit atheist." We bonded.

Shortly thereafter, we ran into two American teenagers of Indian descent who had no packs and appeared to be lost. We asked if they were okay. They told us that their parents were letting them walk ahead but their mom walked really, really slow and they thought they had passed the café in which they were to meet. I offered to text their parents that all was good and to stay with them. They accepted the text offer but insisted that we keep going. In what seemed like no time, we arrived at the relatively bland Palas de Rei and parted company to get lunch and check into our rooms but promised to meet for Mass at 6 pm at the Church of Santiago de Alba XII for the Feast of Corpus Christi. After a quiet lunch with Jameson during which our discussions got deeper as we realized our days together on the pilgrimage were coming to a close (only three more days to go!), we had a brief siesta before attending Mass where the aisle was decorated in elaborate flower petals in celebration of the feast day.

Flower petals lining the aisle in the in Palas de Rei at the Church of Santiago de Alba XII for the feast of Corpus Christi.

It was also Father's Day and we posted on our blog thanks to both my dad and father-in-law for the positive influences they had been in our lives. My father instilled in me a love of walking with Boy Scout hiking trips to Dolly Sods, West Virginia, family outings to Shenandoah National Park, and nightly walks throughout the affluent suburb of Pittsburgh where I grew up, especially the night before trash collection (I know I embarrassed him but Mt. Lebanon had great trash picking!). My father-in-law welcomed me into his family when I married Karyn and has treated me like a son ever since. I have learned so much from him and fondly recalled how much he appreciates the beauty of nature, noticing little things that I would have missed, like the time we caught a flounder and the minnow we used as bait was intact in its stomach, or the time we were admiring a beautiful piece of furniture and he wondered aloud what kind of tree the wood had come from. There is a saying quoted in our guidebook that summed up the impact that family had on us during the pilgrimage.

> *Walking I am listening to a deeper way.*
> *Suddenly, all my ancestors are behind me.*
> *Be still they say.*
> *Watch and listen.*
> *You are the result of the love of thousands.*
> *- Linda Hogan*

After Mass, Robin, Julie and their daughters invited Jameson, Eric, and me out to their plush accommodations on a farm with a swimming pool and gourmet chief. When you're on day 19 of a 21-day, 300-mile hike, you don't pass up such an invitation! To get there we had to take a taxi. It was the first car we had gotten into since the car ride from Biarritz to Saint Jean, and it felt very odd to see the world zooming by outside the windows. As promised, their lodgings were on an elaborate farm estate and we had a gourmet dinner and great discussion. With the sun finally setting and the clock nearing 10 pm, we got the same taxi back to town and retired for the evening. Eric was staying at the same Pension, Pension Barcelona, and we agreed to start early the next day given the continued heat. Even with the window open and the sun down the temperature in our room never dropped below the mid 80's—a temperature even a cold shower could not ease!

Chapter 21

The never ending road to Ribadiso

As was becoming increasingly typical, we woke early (5:30 am) and were hiking before sunrise. Eric joined us having again portaged his pack. Because Eric did not know where he was staying that night, he sent his bags to the hotel we had reserved, Pension Ribadiso. Eric and I talked shop sharing stories and viewpoints as fellow physicians. We stopped at a café after a couple of hours to have breakfast and met up with Gordon from Louisville (nee Nashville) whose feet were hurting so much due to blisters that he had portaged his pack as well. We joked about the economic model of portaging and how it might be interesting to offer a low price at the beginning of the day but the price would increase the closer you got to your destination almost as a penalty for making a poor choice!

At mid-hike we passed through Melide, a town of about 7,500 people. The transition from the rural path to the cobblestone streets of the first section of town were lined with beautiful flowering plants. After trekking through a more industrial area we got to the town center. Vendors were hawking grilled octopus, a local specialty. We were hungry, but the vendors were a little too "in your face" for our liking, and we hiked on, buying some fruit in a local supermarket.

We asked for a restaurant recommendation, but found that they were all closed at this hour—about 10:30 am—too late for breakfast and too early for lunch. We got our credentials stamped in the Sancti Spiritus church in the sacristy and decided to press on. We stopped at a café on the outskirts of town that looked like it was serving, but it only had pastries left over from the morning. We bought what was available. Eating some of this on the patio of the café, we saw perhaps the most ironic logo on the Camino on a pilgrim's hat which read "Antisocial Social Club"!

We continued to struggle with the heat and, without a proper lunch, Jameson started walking a bit in a staggered fashion—a sign I knew meant he was tired and needed food. I was behind him and saw Eric walk up and talk to him following which Eric took Jameson's pack and they hiked on. From my position a couple yards behind them I cried knowing how hard it was for Jameson to receive help. In my mind, I was referencing our conversation near the beginning of our trip when Jameson said he didn't think that he would allow someone else to carry his pack. But, in the instant when he needed it, when a fellow pilgrim had the ability to help (having portaged his pack that morning), he graciously and gratefully accepted help. On that night's blog post Jameson wrote that Eric had asked "Can I take your pack and lift your spirit?" and "…I immediately thought of the conversation my dad and I had. God was giving me a chance to learn some humility and I clearly saw that he wanted me to give my backpack up. My instant thought was 'No, it's only 3 km or so to the next café. I can do this.' But then I thought for a moment and I decided to surrender. He took my pack and I felt much better but was still dizzy and weak until the next food stop."

That next food stop was Café Bar Santiago where we again ran into Gordon, his dad, and some fellow pilgrims whose injuries were mounting. Even though we had less than 30 miles to reach Santiago, we all felt very vulnerable to injury. Small, seemingly trivial things like a sprained ankle or worsening of blisters could thwart our journey even this close to our destination. We were also discouraged about the distance we had traveled and how far we had for the day. The guidebook had said this would be a relatively typical day of 15.5 miles but we were already there according to my iPhone pedometer. We were not sure how much farther we had to hike.

Jameson and Eric (sans shirt) cooling off in río Iso.

Gordon's dad thought it was at least three more miles, but others thought three more kilometers (a huge difference to hungry, tired pilgrims hiking in oppressive heat!). Buoyed by food and hydration, we set out again and after about 45 minutes of hiking crossed an idyllic arched medieval bridge, on the far side of which was Pension Ribadiso, our lodging for the night! I literally couldn't believe it and kept saying "Is this really it?" I was awestruck. We went in and Eric's pack was sitting in the reception area. Eric helped us check in and asked if there was another room—the proprietor shook his head but kept asking us "Tres?" Finally we realized that he was asking us if we wanted a double or triple room—apparently he could accommodate us all in one room but did not have another room on top of that. We couldn't believe our luck yet again and gladly took the triple room which had its own bathroom!

After putting down our packs, we went down to the lovely (and cool!) river, which the bridge spanned, and went in for a dip. It was a popular spot with the fieldtrip group wading in as well. After the heat of the day, it was exactly what we needed! Eric showed us how to capture insects and toss them over to an area where fish would jump out to eat them. The day had really turned around! With Jameson's spirits soaring, Eric showed him how to do laundry in his camping washer (essentially a bag with an agitator), and Jameson did my laundry! We played some cards (Eric knew how to play cribbage) and went across the cobblestone street to a restaurant which was owned by the same person who owned the pension where we were staying. Eric spoke to him and his son, a recent engineering grad, about the business model of running a pension on the Camino (sounded fairly profitable, with about a 5-year return on investment) and contrasted that to his experience running a B&B in Seattle.

While eating, Nicky and Alex, the two American boys of Indian descent whom we saw the day before, came down the path. Eric waved them over, and they sat down, bemoaning how slow their mom and sister were hiking. We ordered more food and hydration. About an hour later, Nicky's mom and sister appeared. Their mom looked rough, and from two doctors' perspective it appeared she was near heat exhaustion. She didn't want to accept our help but finally acquiesced and we ordered more food and drink. Slowly she perked up and was able to contact her husband who had hiked ahead trying to find their hotel. He came back to meet up with them and, after grand introductions (she a radiologist from Boston and he a medical device serial entrepreneur), called a taxi to take them the 1.5 miles or so to their hotel but not before Alex and Nicky asked if they could hike with us tomorrow. With their parents' okay, we made plans to meet up with them at their hotel at 7 am. What a day!

Another sign pointing us on the Way.

Chapter 22
Pedrouzo: The end is near...

We awoke early—not only to meet up with Alex and Nicky but also because of the continuing heat. We got a scant breakfast from the restaurant and hiked a couple of miles to meet up with our new traveling companions. I did not get a hard-boiled egg (*heuvo duro*) at our casa rural so I walked into cafes in Arzúa looking for such and was rewarded! Amazingly, my lack of Spanish was an asset as I stated

Cooling down under shade in a café in Salceda.

simple phrases (e.g., "tres") and pointed to the thing I desired. As I neared the square where we were to meet, Nicky was sitting on the stoop of the hotel, saw me, and jumped up to return to his hotel room to inform his parents that we were here and he was ready to go. We crossed the street and met up with Robin, Julie, Jane, and Kat—Jameson and Eric had beat me there while I was on a quest for *heuvo duro*. We set out. To the Seattle crew, we had two days of seven total to go—so still a significant proportion of nearly one third of their pilgrimage. To Jameson and I, we had two days of twenty-one to go, a much smaller amount of only about 10% of our pilgrimage. This realization weighed on us. While excited about reaching our destination, we were realizing that the journey was the real treat.

Our traveling companions for the end of our pilgrimage. From L to R, Nicky, Jameson, Eric, Robin, Jane, Julie, Kat, Alex, and the author. Smiles, everyone!

The day passed quickly. Alex and Nicky, full of life, peppered us with content ranging from religious beliefs to their experiences in private schools. Jameson and I reflected on how close we were to the end. We were literally treasuring every step. I know this sounds bizarre (we had hiked hundreds of thousands of steps by this time), but we were quickly realizing that the end was near, for good or for bad. We hiked through beautiful Eucalyptus forests providing welcome shade. We stopped for food at Salceda in a café that had bras hanging from the rafters. Jameson took a picture of me smiling under their shade. Weighing on my mind was news from home that my Uncle Vince had suffered a stroke and was in critical condition in an intensive care unit. That night, reflecting on the fragility of life, I posted an age-old adage that one should laugh, cry, and love every day. We took perhaps my favorite picture of the entire Camino—our second "Godspell" posse with smiles on our faces exemplifying that love.

Sooner that we had imagined, we arrived in Pedrouzo, a "way town," with no real city center and hotels lined up on the main road leading to Santiago. Having arranged for another triple room, Eric, Jameson, and I checked in while Alex and Nicky hung out in the air conditioned reception area. Hungry, we asked the proprietor for a restaurant recommendation—they suggested a place that was renowned for cooking meat on a hot stone placed in the middle of the table. We were the only pilgrims who had arrived for lunch, and the meal was AWESOME—perhaps the best of the entire journey. We savored the company as well as the food.

Carne on a stone in Pedrouzo with (from left to right) Alex, Nicky, and Jameson.

True to form, Alex and Nicky's parents were slow to arrive. We checked the boys into their hotel and then headed to ours for a shower and to do laundry. Jameson and I headed to Mass and on the way my cousin Mary, Uncle Vince's youngest daughter, called to discuss his situation. Mary and I were born only four days apart and went to college together. When we talk, the years apart melt away. Uncle Vince was at least responding but was adamant that he did not want extraordinary measures including a feeding tube. I offered hope that perhaps it was not as bad as it sounded, but deep in my heart I knew that it was. I teared up while talking to my cousin. Jameson was again patient with me.

I toiled through another Mass in Spanish with my mind wandering frequently to my Uncle's condition. And then, after the Liturgy, the priest switched to English and told us something I needed to hear. He said the Camino is not the ultimate pilgrimage—the ultimate pilgrimage is the journey to heaven. And, while the Camino can help us appreciate that ultimate pilgrimage, we should not confuse the two. WOW! A necessary reminder that our earthly journey does not have to include a physical pilgrimage. A great reminder that while we were trying to improve our relationship with God through this journey, we could improve that relationship from anywhere as effectively as we could walking 300 miles in northern Spain!

That night we traveled again to Robin and Julie's fancy hotel a couple kilometers back from where our lodging was located. Riding in a car was again a strange experience. We had a lovely dinner and the cook gave us a ride back to our lodging in Pedrouzo. The night was long and hot with a barking dog and then a rooster keeping us up, but it was our last night on the Way…

Altar in church in Pedrouzo where the priest reminded us that the Camino is not the true pilgrimage—our lives' journey to heaven is!

Chapter 23
Santiago de Compostela

We started the last day of the journey with great anticipation and rose before the sun in a last effort to avoid the heat. Eric portaged his bag and headed to Alex and Nicky's hotel because they wanted to join us during our last day's hike. The Way quickly headed out of town and through beautiful tree-lined paths. I was in a great mood, but Jameson was beating himself up again. I tried to keep him positive but was unable to turn his mood around.

The Way coursed around one of the airport runways where we would be departing in just a few days. We met the youngest pilgrim, a toddler who could not have been more

Arriving on the outskirts of Santiago de Compostela.

than five years old who was part of a family from Japan. We stopped at the top of a hill overlooking the city where a monument commemorates the visit of Saint Pope John Paul II and got a snack and a drink. Moving on, Eric (sans pack) and Alex had an impromptu push-up contest in the middle of the road and picked up the pace in an effort to make the noon pilgrim Mass in Santiago leaving Jameson and me with Nicky and the rest of the Seattle crew. We hit the city limits, and I was on the verge of tears. We wove through an industrial section and then into the city. My tears turned to surprise as the familiar "Buen Camino" greetings we had heard so often during the past three weeks were absent. I suspected that the residents of this city had seen so many pilgrims that we were part of the background and no greeting was necessary. My mood soured—perhaps the first time both Jameson and I were down. I tried to lift myself up as I took in the sights, sounds, and smells of the city.

We entered the old part of the city and were overwhelmed by crowds of tourists and street vendors hawking cheap souvenirs. We lost the Way in the traffic and competing signs. We zig-zagged towards the spire of the Cathedral and finally arrived. Truth be told, it was very anticlimactic. I am not sure what we expected, but it wasn't this indifference from the crowd. I felt like yelling out "Hey, we just hiked 300 miles to get here!" but knew it would do no good. I thought back to the priest's comments from the prior night and the old adage that the journey is the goal itself. Unfortunately, we had just missed the noon Mass and the Cathedral was undergoing renovations to the façade. We checked into our hotel, a converted monastery, and found our room on the 2nd floor where we used the restroom and shower. Our room was adjacent to a very large common area where I sat and caught up on email. Unfortunately, the news was not good. Uncle Vince had passed away overnight. I cried for what seemed like a half hour. It was somehow fitting that our pilgrimage had ended the same day his life journey ended.

Hunger brought me back to reality and we connected with our traveling mates over lunch following which we took a siesta. It didn't seem real. Were we really done? We awoke in time to tour the Cathedral and venerate the remains of St.

The remains of St. James under the altar in the Cathedral in Santiago.

James, which sit in a surprisingly small silver box under the back part of the altar. With a little more than an hour until Mass, we realized there were priests hearing confession. Both Jameson and I went, and I confessed that I didn't enjoy the journey as much as I thought I should have and shared the advice from the priest of the previous evening. My penance was to do something nice for my wife in appreciation of her supporting me on the journey.

We recognized fellow pilgrims from Tennessee, who let us know that the giant thurible (incense burner) would be swung from the rafters at Mass that evening supported by a generous donation from Japanese tourists. They told us the best place to sit and we set up shop. After Mass—again in Spanish!—the spectacle of the thurible burner took place and did not disappoint. Picture a backyard chimenea swinging from the rafters of a church with flames visible coming out of the grated door! (Clearly, this would never be allowed in litigation happy United States.) The priest asked people not to take pictures or videos but his request had the exact opposite effect as hundreds of spectators pulled out cell phones. On the way back to the hotel, where we had all agreed to meet for dinner, we stopped at the pilgrim's office to get our official certificate.

After a pilgrim's meal at our hotel with both the Boston crew and the Seattle crew, the kids played cards for hours. No one wanted the evening to end. We departed for our hotels with plans to take a city tour the next day.

The giant thurible swinging over the crowd after Pilgrim's Mass in Santiago.

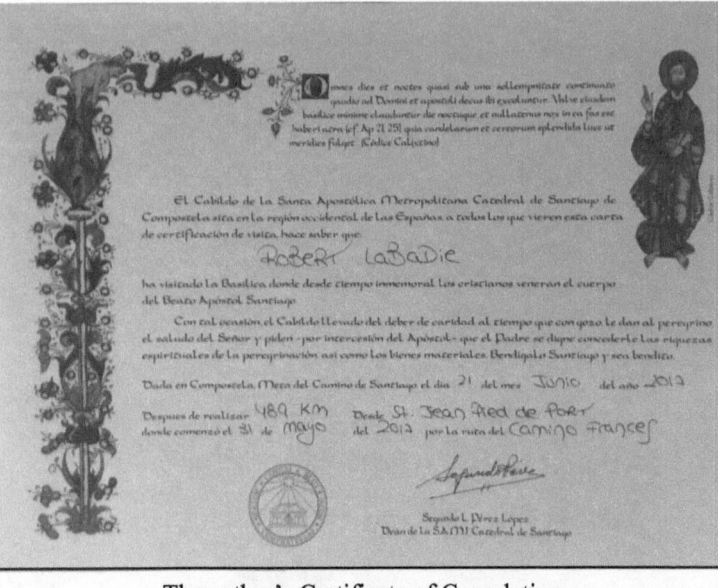

The author's Certificate of Completion.

Chapter 24
Exploring Santiago

For the first time in weeks we did not set an alarm. While it was hot, we slept surprisingly well, woke late (8 am-ish) and had a pilgrim's breakfast. A special English Mass in one of the side chapels was set for 10 am, and we and both the Seattle and Boston groups attended. Jameson and I arrived a bit early and were asked to do the first reading and the responsorial psalm. The priest was the same one who I had gone to confession with the day before. His homily in English (YEAH!) used the analogy of the yellow arrows leading along the

Final Mass (in English by a Brazilian priest) in a side chapel of the Cathedral.

path to Santiago which we had seen throughout our pilgrimage with Christ and the Eucharist leading us to heaven. When intentions were asked, I prayed for the repose of Uncle Vince's soul. Communion was remarkable because the priest held the Eucharist with such care as he distributed the consecrated Hosts.

Julie and Robin and their kids were staying at the Parador and were told it was the finest hotel in all of Spain. Through the concierge, they had arranged a tour of the city for the afternoon. Until then, we ambled around the city, shopped, and had a delicious lunch. The private tour was outstanding with sights that we would have never found on our own including the **"cookie nuns,"** nuns of the Monasterio e iglesia de San Pelayo who bake almond cookies which are highly sought after especially near festival times. I'm not sure I could find the same spot—the Internet tells me it is located on Via Sacra—but I certainly remember the process: walk up to the barred window, ring the bell, wait for a nun

Tastes, smells, sights and sounds in Santiago. Left, a cloistered nun selling almond cookies from a window in their monastery. Right, a public symphony performance in a plaza outside the Cathedral.

to appear, pay for your order and enjoy! We saw beautiful chapels, the skinniest street in the city, the University, street festivals, and even a seemingly impromptu symphony performance. We stopped for tapas—our last meal together. Parting ways, we promised to keep in touch but realized we would likely never have another experience like this one.

The next morning, after one last pilgrim's meal—a breakfast where we were reunited with the Australian crew with whom we had shared the birthing of the calf—we packed up, left our trekking poles at the front desk for re-purposing because they would not clear airport security, and asked the concierge to call a taxi cab. One last picture from an Australian pilgrim who was happy to take it (she was an MD as well!) and off to the airport where we saw the Seattle crew who were on the same flight to Paris. When we landed in Paris, we hugged and said a final good bye. It was done.

Pilgrim's breakfast in converted monastery in Santiago.

A final photo of Jameson (left) and the author in front of the Cathedral in Santiago before departing to the airport.

Chapter 25

Next days and weeks

When we arrived in Paris we were overwhelmed by the mass of humanity. I went to a professional conference while Jameson holed up in the hotel room sleeping. Our plane ride home was delayed and we missed our connection in Atlanta, and I quickly returned to my pre-Camino level of anxiety and anger when things did not go according to plan. In rushing through security in Atlanta, Jameson tripped on his unlaced boots and almost knocked out his front teeth. I

A screenshot of the author's iPhone's pedometer showing miles (y-axis) and days (x-axis). From June 1 to June 21 we averaged 15 miles per day with a peak near 20 miles on June 15.

felt guilty for rushing him and for not trusting that ~~the Camino~~ Life provides but not always in the way I might like.

When we arrived in Nashville (only one hour late—the airline had booked us on the next flight), we were greeted by my other sons holding signs made by them and their friends. My favorite was "Welcome home—only eight more miles to walk!" implying that we were walking home from the airport! That would have been on top of the 300 miles we had hiked in 21 days, averaging 15 miles per day tipping out at 19+ miles on that fateful day to Triacastela. We reunited with loved ones include third son, Aidan, who had been about 100 miles south of us on a high school exchange program in Salamanca, Spain—close, but in reality a five day hike!

It was very difficult trying to explain to even my family and closest friends the experience we had—one of the reason I decided to write it down! Perhaps the closest I could get was telling them it was like trying to explain to a couple pondering marriage what the experience would be like or a couple expecting a child what the experience would be like—I could go over logistics but the reality was that each experience would be unique and only understood after living through it. The morning after we arrived home, I walked to Mass. People thought I was crazy, but I so desired walking! (Jameson slept in a little and drove.) At Mass, we met a fellow parishioner who had also done the Camino. It was like we were in a secret society and little needed to be said—we understood each other.

Going back to work was tough. Colleagues were either genuinely happy that I had the experience or jealous that I took so much time off. I found daily choices (e.g. what clothes to wear, what to eat) difficult as I hadn't made such choices in over a month with only two sets of clothes and limited menu options. I felt guilty about all the clothes in my closest and our large house. I promised myself that I would not let the experience not change me, perhaps ignorant to the fact that it already had profoundly changed me.

Aidan (left), Matthew (middle), and Zachary (right) welcoming us at the airport with signs suggesting we would walk home!

Afterword

Since our return, I had a gnawing desire to share our blog with a dear friend, John Raub, who had lived a remarkable life. A fellow graduate of the University of Notre Dame, he became a parish priest in Youngstown, Ohio after failing to qualify for the seminary in his hometown of Cleveland. After a distinguished career as a teacher and administrator, he felt a calling to become a monk. He became a Trappist monk residing in the Abbey of Our Lady of Gethsemani outside Bardstown, Kentucky (the abbey made famous by Thomas Merton whose time at Gethsemani overlapped with John's) for 28 years before feeling the call to leave the monastery—a call he once told me was just as strong as the call to enter the monastery. With few family members still living, he moved to Clarksville, Tennessee, a military base in close proximity to Gethsemani, where he had many friends whom he had met as the retreat director at the monastery. Living out of a friend's basement, he integrated into their lives, following which he met and married a widow.

I had come to know John and Anne because John had become a patient of mine for run-of-the mill allergies. He happened to come to our office and noted a short biography of me posted on the wall, and he quickly made the Notre Dame connection. For the past ten years, John and I had written, called, and met in person about three to four times a year discussing spiritual matters. He had written and published a book in 1992 loosely based on *A Course in Miracles* entitled *Who Told You You Were Naked?* which had received critical success. One of the many spiritual lessons I learned from John was the concept of *felix culpa* referred to in Chapter 15. This theological concept states that God produces good things even out of apparent bad things with the classic example being the Crucifixion—that without Jesus' death, the resurrection, the central concept of Christianity, would not be.

I wanted to share how much of an impact John had made on our lives—for crying out loud, our whole day lost outside Ponferrada I thought about it! Knowing that John's computer skills were a bit lacking, I printed out a copy of the blog and mailed it to his house and eagerly awaited his telephone call, which typically would come three to four days after I mailed him a letter. The last time we spoke was in April, when I shared with him that Jameson would be attending our shared alma mater, Notre Dame. The telephone call never came and I tried calling. I had two different numbers, a home number and a cell number, and I recall John telling me one was disconnected, but I couldn't remember which one. I couldn't get through on either line. Knowing that he was a parishioner at Immaculate Conception Catholic Church in Clarksville, I called the parish office and was told that his funeral had occurred a couple of weeks back.

He had finally gotten his wife into an assisted-living facility to help care for her progressive Alzheimer's disease. He was living alone for the first time and either had a stroke or a simple fall only to be discovered days later alive but near death, which came—mercifully—shortly thereafter. To try to affect closure, I scheduled a meeting with the parish priest there, Fr. Steve Wolf, who had been our parish priest in Nashville just a couple years earlier. On a Saturday morning in August of 2017, we celebrated John's life sharing writings he had shared with us. I'm convinced John was with us.

After-afterword

A couple weeks after we got home, I got a What'sApp message from Frank that he had finished on July 3rd and journeyed on to Finisterre once thought to be the end of the world where the Way intersects the Pacific Ocean. Jameson and I thought that was the end of the good news, but then we got another message that Pablo had returned to the Camino and reached Santiago on September 23rd!

Frank's photo from Finisterre where the Way meets the Pacific Ocean.

Pablo finishing September 23rd!

Closure

In trying to wrap up my reflections on the Camino, I re-read the last section of John Brierley's guidebook entitled *Returning Home: Reflections...* Amazing to me, John Brierley closes with a reflection attributed to Marianne Williamson and taken from *A Course in Miracles*, the source which motivated John Raub's *Who Told You You Were Naked?* The message was elegantly delivered by Nelson Mandela in his *Freedom Speech* (Breirley, page 285).

Our deepest fear is not that we are inadequate.
Our deepest fear is that we are powerful beyond measure.
It is our Light, not our darkness, that most frightens us.

We ask ourselves, who am I to be brilliant, gorgeous, talented, and fabulous?
Actually, who are you not to be? You are a child of God.
Your playing small doesn't serve the world.
There's nothing enlightened about shrinking so that other people won't feel insecure around you.

We are born to make manifest the Glory of God that is within us.
It's not just in some of us; it's in everyone.

And as we let our Light shine, we unconsciously give other people permission to do the same.
As we are liberated from our own fear, our presence automatically liberates others.

John Brierley's guide suggests a self-assessment before and after the Camino. Truth be told, I skimmed over the self-assessment prior to the trip but found myself, some three months out, coming back to certain questions, particularly, the following:

> *What do you see as the primary purpose of your life?*
>
> *Are you working consciously towards fulfilling that purpose?*
>
> *How clear are you on your goal and the right direction for you at this time?*
>
> *How will you recognize resistance to any changes that might be required of you?*

Coming home, I have gotten into the same ruts I recognized hiking over the Pyrenes; but, I recognize this more clearly now. I have become too complacent with the ease of my life; but I recognize the stirring to not let this happen, and, when faced with an opportunity to change this, I think I do more now than pre-Camino. Perhaps most importantly, I think I recognize the miracles that happen every day. Prior to the Camino, I perhaps missed these miracles staring into my cell phone and lost in the busy-ness of life. Post-Camino, I am not immune to this, but perhaps a little less susceptible and try to laugh, cry, and love on a daily basis—now that is a full day (paraphrasing Jimmy Valvano)!

I will close with the quote that brought John Raub and his parish priest, Steve Wolf, together. It is a quote from Cardinal Emmanuel Célestin Suhard, a French priest and Archbishop of Paris from 1940-1949.

> *To be a witness does not consist in engaging in propaganda, nor even in stirring people up, but in being a living mystery.*
> ***It means to live in such a way that one's life would not make sense if God did not exist.***

Live, laugh, love. Enjoy everyday miracles. Make your own pilgrimage, whatever form it might take.

Buen Camino!

Robert Labadie

September 2017

www.ingramcontent.com/pod-product-compliance
Lightning Source LLC
Chambersburg PA
CBHW021150080526
44588CB00008B/289